IN THE WAY

What Others Are Saying About *In the Way*

"*In the Way* is an invitation to re-think, re-imagine, and dare I say re-dream what God wants to do in and through your church. As a church leader passionate about growing the kingdom, Damian's approach to creating a disciple-multiplying movement will not only change the way you think about church, it might just spark a movement that transforms your city!"

Jon Ferguson, Co-Founding Pastor of Community Christian Church, Chicagoland, Illinois, Co-Founder of NewThing, author of *Finding Your Way Back to God: 5 Awakenings to Your New Life* and *B.L.E.S.S.: 5 Everyday Ways to Love Your Neighbor and Change the World.*

"*In the Way* is an invaluable resource for those interested in multiplicative disciple making. Not only is the tool valuable for skill building but his quick trot through church history is worth the price of the book itself! You won't just read this book, you'll put it on the bookshelf where you can find it easily because it will be a handy reference, full of illustrations and coaching topics."

Roy Moran, Sr. Pastor of Shoal Creek Community Church, Kansas City, Kansas, and author of *Spent Matches: Igniting the Signal Fire for the Spiritually Dissatisfied*

"Damian's book is a must-read for everyone wanting to catalyze movements of disciples making disciples and churches planting churches. He contrasts CAWKI (Church As We Know It) with a multiplicative, disciple-making strategy and makes a compelling case for how we should pursue multiplication if we really desire for all to hear and all to know! This book will probably step on your toes, but in a much needed way. I believe you'll walk away with a holy discontent with CAWKI and an increased passion to do whatever it takes to see a multiplication movement in your city!"

Chris Galanos, Sr. Pastor of Experience Life Church, Lubbock, Texas, and author of *From Megachurch to Multiplication: A Church's Journey Toward Movement*

"If I had the skills, I would have written this book. Thankfully Damian Gerke did and did it very well. I have a long history with, and deep empathy for, people working tirelessly to strengthen the legacy church. However, I am fully committed to the Disciple-Multiplying Movement (DMM) strategy that Damian so carefully unpacks within these pages. The DMM strategy began with Christ's own ministry. If you are struggling to understand how Christ's model for discipleship looks in the world today, this book will walk you through the process. Even if you are actively involved in a DMM, this book will give you tools, context, and encouragement to effectively foster this conversation with others."

John Heerema, CEO of Biglife International, Inc.

"From within the context of the North American church, Damian Gerke has given us a valuable insight into how Disciple Multiplication Movements can become a reality here in the U.S. I highly recommend to you this thoughtful and engaging guide to following *In the Way* of Jesus."

David Garrison, missions pioneer, author of *A Wind in the House of Islam: How God is Drawing Muslims Around the World to Faith in Jesus Christ* and *Church Planting Movements: How God Is Redeeming a Lost World*

"*In the Way* is one of the most unique books I've read in recent years. It hits you at a strategic level with a laser focus on what's most important. What makes this book so powerful is how it addresses discipleship at a practical level with clear insight on how to make disciple-making disciples. It's deeply emotional, filling you with hope and expectation that Christ's body can truly come together in unity for the cause of God's Kingdom. As both a vocational pastor and ministry leader in a secular environment, I've come away challenged, convicted, and repentant, and at the same time, motivated, encouraged, and inspired. It is a must-read for pastors, church leaders, and anyone who wants to see the church achieve the mission our Savior gave us."

Kevin Weaver, CEO of Network 211,
CEO/Co-Founder of The Warrior's Journey

"This moving and profound book is for those who love Jesus and his church but realize we are not close to fulfilling the potential for which he died and rose again. It is for those who believe every follower of Jesus can be an active and reproducing disciple-maker but need practical insight into how to be and make such disciples. It is for those who dream of—but have a hard time believing—reports of disciples reproducing exponentially. It is for those who want a strong biblical/theological discussion of the patterns of disciple- and church-multiplication. It is for those who want extensive practical help in disciple-making, in both resources and relational connections with experienced practitioners from a variety of organizations. I am thrilled to commend this book—and will do so to all of our personnel and to church leaders I know around the world."

Kent Parks, President and CEO, Beyond

"I've heard many church leaders jokingly say, 'Lead, follow, or get out of the way.' But, what if it's true that we as church leaders have adopted elements of church leadership that have gotten 'in the way?' *In the Way* takes a hard look at how we have gotten stuck and what it's going to take to move forward as a thriving movement of Christ followers. Lord help us get out of your Way, and walk *In the Way!*"

Guy Caskey, Movements Pastor, Wood's Edge Community Church,
The Woodlands, Texas, and author of *Making Him L.O.R.D.:*
Living Out Reproducible Discipleship

"I've known Damian to be a follower of Jesus who thoughtfully and compassionately desires the church to be as Jesus intended. *In the Way* is a thought-provoking examination of where we are and where we could and should go together—the better way of Jesus."

Jason Dukes, Church Multiplication Minister,
Brentwood Baptist Church, Brentwood, Tennessee, and author
of *Live Sent: You Are a Letter* and *Beyond My Church: Thinking and*
Living So That the World Might Know

IN THE WAY

Church As We Know It
Can Be a Discipleship Movement (Again)

Damian Gerke

In the Way: Church as We Know It Can Be a Discipleship Movement (Again)

Cover Design: Amy Allen-Harris

ISBN: 978-1-7330962-9-4

Printed and bound in the United States of America

Published by Network211 in partnership with Three Clicks Publishing.
3003 E. Chestnut Expressway Ste 2001
Springfield, MO 65802

network211.org

To Jesus the Christ,
the Shepherd and Overseer of my soul

Contents

Acknowledgements

If you want to go fast, go alone.
If you want to go far, go together.

The longer I live the more true this proverb becomes. It's as true in the production of a book as anything else. The author gets his/her name on the cover, but there are so many who contribute to the content that to list only one person's name is laughable.

First, constant thanks go to Cheryl, my life partner and lover. You keep me honest and humble as you simultaneously help make me become the man I long to be. I love you more than I can ever communicate!

Next, my deepest and greatest thanks go to my partners in ministry at 1Body Church: Lee and Stacy Wood, Jay and Terri Fechtel, and Dominic and Debbie Sputo, along with the entire ministry team and leaders who have given their all to Jesus and His mission. It is refreshing and humbling to be in a group of leaders who mutually submit to one another in love, who play off each other's strengths and shore up each other's weaknesses in a way that doesn't diminish or demean. I've never been in a leadership team with this level of interdependence. Each of your voices, passions, and insights found their way into the words in this book in so many ways. Each of you is a gift and a joy to work with! Thank you for your service to the cause.

Special thanks to all the leaders and disciples that are part of the mission of 1Body Church. Your steadfast faith and commitment to launch and grow disciple-multiplying movements inspire me!

Thanks to my personal supporters who've given of their time and money to see this vision come to fruition. I had my version of a burning bush, told you the story, and you bought in! There's absolutely no way this book sees the light of day without each and every one of you!

Thanks to Chris Galanos and Roy Moran for allowing me to tell just a bit of the story behind your churches. Thank you, brothers, for your own level of dedication and faithfulness in pursuing the making and multiplying of disciples. I pray for you and your churches, and may they be cities of light on the hills they've been planted, to the glory of God!

I also want to acknowledge the many DMM church practitioners around the U.S. and around the world that are moving forward out of your holy discontent at the status quo in response to the calling each of you has received. You've responded in faith, not knowing the destination but moving out with your tents and belongings to go to the land God will show you. I applaud you!

Special thanks go to my coach mentor, Kevin Weaver, and the team at Three Clicks Publishing and Network211. Y'all are amazing, and the kingdom impact you are having is phenomenal.

Thanks as well to Amy Allen-Harris for the creative design on the cover. Once again, Amy, a home run! Your gifts as a designer are topped only by your faith in Jesus and your service to his church.

Finally, it's impossible to write a book about disciple-multiplying movements without acknowledging the pioneers that have gone before us. You quickly come to the realization that today's conversations on this topic are the fruit of their faithfulness and devotion to Jesus. They blazed a wilderness ministry trail that is now the wide and level path we explore. They entrepreneurially re-invented a wheel whose design had long been lost, at a time when the model and methods were neither clear nor convenient. They have more kingdom impact than most pastors in the West could even dream of, yet they have diligently and quietly served out of the limelight for decades. Many are living, and many have fallen asleep and are already with the Lord. Only Jesus knows them all, but there are a few who've had significant impact on me personally. I list them here as representatives of all those who've faithfully gone before us: George and Denny Patterson, Curtis and Debie Sergeant, Ying and Grace Kai, Stan and Kay Parks, Bill Smith, and Steve and Laura Smith. Thank you all for your model of hearing and obeying, and may God bless and multiply the fruit of your faith and ministry as you "look forward to the day of God and speed its coming" (1 Pet. 3:12).

Foreword

By Curtis Sergeant

For those of you who do not know Damian Gerke, I would like to say a few words of introduction. Damian is a measured man, a thoughtful man, a careful man. He is not given to bombastic statements or exaggeration. I tell you this so you will hear the message of this book in the spirit in which it was written. The message of this book is prophetic in nature, but not a prophetic message delivered with a doomsday tone or in a threatening manner.

Damian loves the church in its many expressions. He knows Christ died for the church and loves it. He knows it is the body of Christ and the bride of Christ. He wants the very best for the church. That is why he wrote this book. To adapt a phrase from the Lord's Prayer, Damian would pray, "Your Kingdom come, Your will be done, in Your church as it is in heaven." That is the spirit behind this book.

Over the centuries, the church has morphed and adapted to such an extent that many of the key purposes and functions of church as God intended, have been effectively lost or at least severely blunted. We need for the church to reclaim those purposes and accomplish those functions in order that we can collectively be the people the Lord intends us to be, and do what He intends for us to do.

Most people have a bent toward trying to improve the systems they live and work in by fine-tuning and tinkering. Some have the insight and foresight to question those systems and propose alternatives. A few have the courage to step out and do what they can to replace and renew those systems. This book intends to call forth those with such courage to remake church in our time.

Damian is only asking us to do what he has done himself. He has devoted himself to serving the church and the Kingdom for decades.

As he has continually grown in his realization of the shortcomings of those efforts, he has stepped out of the safety of familiar patterns into expressions which more effectively fulfill the biblical mandates in our current world. I urge you to consider the challenges presented in this book and then make the sacrifices and take the risks to implement the proposed changes.

There are already plenty of people who have experienced the potential in the approaches which this book promotes. The earliest efforts took place among extremely unreached people groups in "restricted access" nations in the early 1990s. Today, there are over seventy-three million people in churches using these approaches, and there are examples in every continent and every type of cultural and religious environment. The "tipping point" has been passed and the momentum of growth is now literally exponential. I have had the privilege of being involved in a number of such movements around the world and observing many others as part of the leadership of 24:14 (2414now.net) which is now serving as a community of practitioners around the world. This not only can happen, but has happened.

Up to this point, practitioners of these approaches have included mainly "innovators" and "early adopters" but it is time now for the movement to become mainstream and begin to involve "early majority" people. Up to now the practitioners have largely been apostolic (pioneer) and prophetic types, but it is time for the movements to begin to mature and incorporate more of the other equipping leaders (evangelists, shepherds, and teachers) in key leadership. This is critical if these expressions of church are to be complete and balanced and play an increasingly prominent role in the overall advance of the Kingdom. We are all needed.

One of the significant results of these approaches in just the last few years is that for the first time in quite a while, the percentage of disciples of Christ as a part of global population is increasing. The runaway increase in the number of people in the world has made such progress incredibly difficult in recent years. At last there is hope for—and an actual beginning in—outpacing population growth with kingdom growth. When coupled with amazing progress in the past fifteen years in getting work started among every ethnolinguistic people group on the planet, this means we can reasonably conceive finishing the task of the Great Commission in the foreseeable future. If those small beginnings in many places can be rapidly spread and deepened with these multiplicative approaches, then both qualitative and quantitative progress will be extreme. Doing so will require commitment and focus and sacrifice on our part.

Let us together do all we can to be a part of the generation that completes that task assigned to us by the Lord. Let us be in tune with the moment-by-moment instructions of the Holy Spirit. Let us labor together in unity and love. Let us love the Lord with all our heart, mind, soul, and strength. Let us seek to make disciples who obey all Christ commanded until the knowledge of the glory of the Lord covers the earth as the waters cover the sea.

Your partner in the battle,
Curtis Sergeant

Introduction

The church.

It's "God's household ... the pillar and foundation of truth" (1 Tim. 3:15). It is "Christ's body, the fullness of him who fills everything in every way" (Eph. 1:23). It's described as the bride of Christ, whom he loved and died for so that she might be made glorious, without spot or wrinkle, holy and blameless (Eph. 5:25–27). It is the object lesson for God's eternal purpose to display his "manifold wisdom ... to the rulers and authorities in the heavenly realms" (Eph. 3:10).

The church is the people of Christ, a label Jesus and the New Testament writers used by redeeming the common Greek word *ekklesia*: a gathering of those summoned to discuss civil matters of state. In the context of Christ and his followers, it describes the collective relationships of "those summoned" in Christ to discuss matters of his kingdom, from two or more in a local setting up to the entirety of believers across the globe.

The mental picture associated with the word "church"—for Christians and non-Christians alike—has largely been solidified in the West for well over a millennia. While the expressions and forms of the church have ebbed, flowed, and morphed over the years, the common interpretation of "church" remains practically unchanged.

This organizational identity—and how we participate in it—is the focus of this book.

First and foremost, I want to communicate my intent. This book is not an attack or critique. I have given the best years of my adult life and much of my worldly wealth for the sake of the local and universal church, and I'm not about to change that priority. I've written this book primarily with church leaders and pastors in mind, those who've made similar sacrifices and commitment to see Jesus' bride flourish. I trust you will understand my sentiment and where I'm coming from.

I honor those who also serve to prosper and grow the church. My hope is not to divide or polarize; in fact, it's quite the opposite: My hope is to partner. I want to create conversation that develops and strengthens unity, and establishes a common ground around the mission and purpose of the church. I believe there is a way to reduce the division that currently exists across the many denominations and theological camps we have segmented ourselves into.

Secondly, while it is not a critique, it is an examination of how the church can be transformed—to become more of what it could be (and used to be) and to become less of what makes the church ineffective in its mission.

I see an opportunity for the church, one that shouldn't be viewed as threatening. In fact, the vast majority of congregations could apply the elements and strategies presented in this book without impacting their programming, dedicating significant finances, or diverting staff responsibilities. And the content of this book is applicable to new church starts. In short: This book is about having additional ministry options to consider.

That said, transformation is change—which by nature involves risks and unknowns. While the programming and finances in your church may not be challenged, your perception of "church" (along with how you function in it) very likely will be. The mental picture generated by that word has been solidified for many centuries, so it's often assumed by many (most?) that church must have a certain form to be genuine. In fact, I would argue that the church has adopted elements of secular culture throughout its history that have gradually shaped it into its current form. While many of these elements are amoral—neither good nor bad—they have impacted the church's ministry effectiveness.

The content of this book will address many of those factors. It will also shed light on things long- and widely-held to be essential to the purpose and function of the church; the simple fact is they aren't.

If anything, they get in the way.

The church began as a movement of the gospel. In roughly 300 years and amidst intense persecution, it spread across most of the known world at the time, growing from a small band of people until the Roman emperor Constantine legalized Christian worship in AD 313. By the fifth century, Christianity had saturated western Europe, England, and much of north Africa, converting an estimated thirty million people to the faith in what's been described as "the single greatest cultural transformation our world has ever seen."[1]

Jesus' followers in the first century referred to this movement of the gospel as "The Way."[2] This book lays out how we can again be in the Way without being in the way.

So you know where I'm coming from, allow me to summarize my background and perspective. I am a practitioner. I have served in vocational ministry roles in churches throughout the continental U.S. (except the Northeast) and in Canada. I have served in old churches and start-up churches, big churches and small churches, denominationally affiliated and non-denominational churches. That variety has, in my opinion, given me perspective.

I grew up in a devout Catholic home and came to an understanding of Jesus' atoning work on the cross at the age of 24 as I read the Bible for the very first time. God's word spoke to me without anyone around to coach me through the steps to become a believer in Christ. I didn't fully understand what I had just read, but I knew I was forever changed. My guilt instantly and completely vanished, replaced with hope and newness of life; in the blink of an eye, my world was transformed from black, white, and flat to full-color and three-dimensional.

Currently, I am a bivocational leader, working in a variety of roles that include writing, training, leadership coaching for individuals and teams in both marketplace and ministry settings. I also help to lead a network of disciple-making simple churches based in Tampa, Florida, called 1Body Church.

Finally, a request: I ask you to read this book with an open mind. I ask you not to react, but instead to *respond*. It will be easy to dismiss the content because it's different from what you know and practice. If you follow Christ, my hope and conviction is that this book will reveal ways you can be more effective in your faith and in strengthening the church.

I also believe we have an enemy that relishes in expanding our differences beyond their level of importance. Let's not give him a platform to continue his work. Of course, we have wide varieties in our doctrinal and theological stances, worship styles, ordinances, cultural expressions, biblical interpretations, etc. But if we step back far enough to view the entire scene, these differences are actually shades of the same color. They should be viewed as the strength of diversity instead of the shallowness of division.

I point you to Jesus' heartfelt desire for us, expressed in prayer to the Father on his way to the cross:

> "I pray also for those who will believe in me through [my disciples'] message, that all of them may be one, Father, just as you are in me and I am in you. May they also be in us so that the world may believe that you have sent me. I have given them the glory that you gave me, *that they may be one as we are one—I in them and you in me—so that they may be brought to complete unity.* Then the world will know that you sent me and have loved them even as you have loved me" (John 17:20–23, emphasis added).

My hope is that this book helps set the stage for the church (particularly in the West) to discover its next steps, to refocus its calling, capability, and vibrancy, and uncover its opportunity that remains largely untapped. I hope for healthy and productive—not divisive— conversations about what the church should be, and then about what it should do. It would be my greatest joy to see this effort unify and invigorate the church.

Finally, this content is a 30,000-foot flyover of the concepts within. Each chapter easily represents a book-worthy topic, and rightfully requires much more space than is available here to discuss and explain in detail. As such, you may experience a level of frustration that some topics appear glossed over and not fully supported and defended. I ask you for patience and grace in advance and for your understanding that this is merely an introduction to what should be multiple conversations to digest fully.

Let the conversations begin.

Definitions

I will utilize a number of terms and acronyms in this book, which are listed here for convenience. Some of these will shape your understanding of what you'll be reading, so it's important that we all have same meaning in mind when we see these terms.

⅓ʳᵈˢ Group Format — A format for group discussion with three parts: 1) "Look back" on events since the previous meeting, 2) "Look up" to discern God's direction from the Scriptures, and 3) "Look forward" to practice and obey that direction. See Appendix B for a description of this format.

Accountability/Accountable — This term is often loaded with negative associations, in both secular and ministry settings. It often carries a sense of control or blame for wrongdoing, negligence, or culpability. That is not the meaning here. Rather, the intended meaning aligns with the technical definition: Accountability is the obligation of an individual or organization to account for its activities, accept responsibility for them, and to disclose the results in a transparent manner. In the context of disciple-making, it is a mutually agreed upon commitment of each person to be open and transparent about what God is revealing to them and what they intend to do in response. It is not heavy-handed or authoritarian, but rather loving and supportive in the context of a healthy Christian community that allows for mutual support, encouragement, exhortation, correction, training, etc.

APEST — An acronym for the five "gifts" described in Ephesians 4:7–16: Apostles, Prophets, Evangelists, Shepherds, and Teachers. These describe the varied activities of believers who work together to build up the church to unity and spiritual maturity. The passage equates these activities with the individuals who are gifts to the church from Christ himself.

Attractional — A church ministry model built upon the strategy of attracting people into a programmatic element, most typically Sunday morning services, with the expectation they will join and become part of the church's attenders.

Branch (of DMM) — A network of disciples and simple churches that share common traits, such as beginning point, specific training methods and terminology, etc.

CAWKI — You'll see this a lot in this book. It's an acronym for part of the book's title: Church As We Know It. It's a neutral description of the expression of church in our western context. It's in no way intended to mean "cocky" as in being prideful or arrogant. I use it, in part, because I'm fond of acronyms. And, frankly, I must admit that it's simpler to use the acronym than typing all the words out.

CPM — An acronym for Church Planting Movement. See **DMM**.

DMM — This is another acronym you'll see quite often in this book. It stands for Disciple-Multiplying Movement, a rapid and multiplicative increase of disciple-making relationships and/or churches. Usually this occurs within a particular cultural segment or people group as multiple generations of disciples or churches are rapidly formed and grown. There is broad agreement that these movements reach significance and sustainability when there are multiple streams with four generations of churches present.

"DMM" has been variously interpreted and applied over the years as the various streams of movement practitioners have operated. In many ways, it's a term that's still coming into a unified definition. Some have used DMM interchangeably with CPM (Church-Planting Movement), while others see DMM as a specific method of disciple-making with some distinct differences and priorities from other multiplicative movement approaches. Some view CPM as the outcome of a DMM strategy. For simplicity's sake (and with respect to all streams of movement practitioners), throughout this book I will use DMM as an over-arching term that applies to all types of disciple-making methods and approaches that have the intention of producing rapid, multi-generational discipleship multiplication and result in a sustainable movement. See also **Movement**.

Disciple — One who follows and practices Jesus' teachings and lifestyle examples as the highest priority in their life.

Disciple-Making — The process of leading others through an intentional process to understand and live out Jesus' commands, and also includes deliberate preparation and training to prepare them to make another disciple. See also **Discipleship**.

Discipleship — In a Western Christian context the term usually implies the process of leading a Christian to a higher level of maturity through a deeper understanding of biblical and theological knowledge. For the purposes of this book, "discipleship" has a significantly broader meaning. It is the entire process of helping someone follow after Jesus—which includes the steps of profession of faith in Christ and baptism. The discipleship process begins from the first interaction and can begin prior to conversion to faith in Christ. In this book it should be seen as synonymous with disciple-making.

Discovery Bible Study — A group meeting format used in DMM groups to discover God's direction from the Holy Spirit using the Scriptures; similar to the $\frac{3}{3}^{rds}$ format.

Filter — The process of interacting with people to assess and discern their level of responsiveness to Jesus' call to be a disciple and a disciple-maker.

Generation — Subsequent levels in the network of discipleship relationships. For example, Paul was one generation from Jesus.

Timothy was one generation from Paul and two generations from Jesus.

Legacy Church — This is any church that follows the typical Western ministry model primarily of the church in the West. It utilizes all the familiar elements we think of in church, such as Sunday morning worship/teaching service as a primary expression, a designated senior minister, etc. "Legacy" is not a reflection of age, tradition, or worship style.

Movement — The collection of successive generations of disciples (typically four or more generations) resulting from a disciple-making process initiated from a single source; all subsequent generations can point back to its first original generation. Many DMM practitioners define a movement as four generations of disciple-making with four separate streams of churches or discipleship streams that occur over a short period of time and include at least 100 groups or 1,000 people. It should also be recognized that the term "movement" has come into wide usage as a popular term and is being applied toward a number of church-planting efforts and initiatives that are not multiplicative. For the purposes of this book, "movement" is limited to multiplicative disciple-making. See **DMM**.

Multiplication — The process of rapid reproduction of generations of disciples, where subsequent generations continue the disciple-making efforts with such intentionality that each successive generation doubles the number of disciples made. This is distinguished from how the term is used to describe the process of legacy church congregations planting or starting multiple generations of new legacy churches.

Obey/Obedience — In this book I am typically referring to the term used in Jesus' call in Matthew 28:19 to teach others to follow his commands and adopt his priorities and practices. Obedience is one of the key elements of being a disciple. The Greek word for "obey" (*terein*) used in the Great Commission (from the NIV) means *to watch over, guard, keep,* or *observe.*[3] In the context of disciple-making and being a disciple it means to live as Jesus lived, deliberately and faithfully practicing his teachings and way of life. It also means to model his practical dependence upon the Father and his willingness to respond to the promptings and leadings of the Holy Spirit received through reading the Scriptures and prayer. It is in no way intended to imply a legalistic, cultic, or authoritative obligation. Neither does it imply a human-powered spirituality that is void of belief in Christ and love for others. Rather, it is simply having a posture of leaning not on our own understanding, but instead to be willing to hear, receive, and respond (in faith) to practice what the Lord reveals to us through his Word and the promptings of the Holy Spirit.

Simple Church — A church in a disciple-making network, probably best conceived as a node in a network of churches connected together relationally or missionally and not tied to a physical location. "Simple" means it is a gathering of disciples who focus on the bare essentials of faith practice, which typically do not involve a building, staff, property, or significant programming.

Stream (of DMM) — See **Branch (of DMM).**

Part 1:
A Long, Hard Look

A revealing survey of how we organize
and practice church in the West,
an assessment of the outcomes
and an introduction of a different way

1   Is It Working?

There is nothing more deceptive than an obvious fact.

—Arthur Conan Doyle

Is the way we're practicing church in the West working?

It's a closed-ended question, but I'm not really asking for your response; I'm asking for what's *behind* your response. On what basis do we measure the effectiveness of our churches' ministries and programs? What's driving our approach to church and all that goes into it? And is all of it accomplishing what we'd hoped for?

For that matter, *what do* we hope for?

As a devoted Christian, church leader, or pastor, I invite you to make an objective and sober assessment of the way we've been doing church: Should we be satisfied with the returns on the significant investments we've made?

In responding to this question, I find that Western Christians predominantly default to one of three perspectives to determine if their ministry is effective:

- How many people are attending church
- To what degree the church presence is expanding and growing
- The type and quality of the preaching/teaching

In addition to these, I suggest three additional perspectives that should be considered but usually aren't:

- The degree of unity in the church
- The quality of the church as an organization
- The biblical perspective of church

Let's look at each of these, then wrap up with another perspective.

Church and Attendance

Church attendance is the de-facto gauge of the health and status of Christianity in the West. It is the universal yardstick, used by everyone from individual congregations to statistical research organizations. It's common for people to use their personal patterns and frequency of church attendance to describe their level of faith—even if that frequency is once or twice a year, or less. From a secular perspective, it's not unusual for someone to claim Christianity as their belief system simply because they went to church as a child.

We use attendance as a faith metric not just because it's *convenient* to measure, but because in most cases it's one of the few things we *can* measure.

We don't often allow ourselves to consider this, but church attendance in and of itself is actually poorly correlated with spiritual maturity. As an illustration, consider this: Let's assume I visit my doctor weekly. In these visits I hear my doctor promote healthy living, a good diet, the importance of exercise and consistent sleep rhythms. I can even have some important measurements taken, like my weight, blood pressure, etc. Are my frequent doctor visits viable evidence that I'm in good physical condition?

Of course not. At most, it would indicate I visit my doctor more frequently than others. While I might be inspired, encouraged, and even educated on being healthy, it would not measure significant health processes.

Granted, attendance is a valid statistic. But it's only one slice of the picture—and a very narrow slice at that. The deeper concern is we use attendance as a faith metric not just because it's *convenient* to measure, but because in most cases (along with things like membership, donations, and baptisms) it's one of the few things we *can* measure in our current approach to church.

But even when considering attendance, the picture for the church in the West is not trending well. As far back as 2008, The American Church Research Project found that church attendance was not even keeping up with population growth in the U.S.[1] Their data showed a net increase of 303 churches from 2000–2005 (new churches started minus churches that closed). However, this net gain was woefully short of the 3,205 churches needed to keep up with population growth.[2] They also noted that most of the churches increasing in attendance (only 31 percent of all Protestant churches in the U.S.) are doing so because they are in zip codes where the overall population is growing.[3]

Recent data shows an even bleaker picture. The Barna Group's 2020 State of the Church Report indicates that 36 percent fewer American adults attends church weekly in 2020 than in 1993. From 1993–2012, the percentage of U.S. adults attending weekly services averaged at 43 percent. Since then, however, that number has declined steadily. In the last four years (2017–2020) the average number is now at 29 percent.

As disconcerting as the attendance numbers are, the actual state is much worse because it seems that attending church is the only thing Christians do. In the more formational and foundational aspects of faith, Christians in the West are woefully weak. Only 52 percent of born-again Christians shared their faith with someone else in the last year.[4] Twenty percent of Christians rarely or never pray for the spiritual status of others.[5] Only 45 percent read the Bible more than once a week, over 40 percent read their Bible once or twice a month and almost 20 percent never read the Bible. Many claiming to be a Christian also have a weak understanding of major doctrines in the faith. For example:

- One in five evangelical Christians believe there are many ways to get to heaven. Fifty-nine percent believe the Holy Spirit is a force and not a personal being.[6]
- Fifty-nine percent strongly or somewhat agree that Satan is not a living being but is rather a symbol of evil, and another 8 percent were not sure what they believed about him.
- Thirty-nine percent strongly or somewhat agree that Jesus Christ sinned when he lived on the earth, with an additional 6 percent who had no opinion.
- Sixty-one percent strongly agree, somewhat agree, or are undecided with the statement that the Bible, the Koran, and the Book of Mormon are all different expressions of the same spiritual truths.[7]

Studies also show that our church attendance is not making a significant impact on the way Christians live out their faith. From the perspective of non-Christians, only 14 percent of those who self-identify as Christian represent Christlike attitudes and actions (i.e., exhibiting love for others).[8] In his research-based book *unChristian*, David Kinnaman states that 84 percent of young non-Christians say they know a Christian personally, yet only 15 percent say the lifestyles of those believers are noticeably different in a good way. Kinnaman sums up how those outside of Christianity view Christians:

"The primary reason outsiders feel hostile toward Christians, and especially conservative Christians, is not because of any specific theological perspective. What they react negatively to is our 'swagger,' how we go about things and the sense of self-importance we project …

"In our national surveys we found the three most common perceptions of present-day Christianity are antihomosexual (an image held by 91 percent of young outsiders), judgmental (87 percent), and hypocritical (85 percent). These 'big three' are followed by the following negative perceptions, embraced by a majority of young adults: old-fashioned, too involved in politics, out of touch with reality, insensitive to others, boring, not accepting of other faiths, and confusing. When they think of the Christian faith, these are the images that come to mind."[9]

The COVID pandemic has also thrown the focus on church attendance into question. Virtually overnight, church attendance was taken away as a viable metric as churches scrambled for ways to remain connected to their congregations that now couldn't congregate. The effort to connect with individuals and families remotely who were now scattered and shut in at home revealed a level of vulnerability never before anticipated. The church has become over-dependent on gathering its members into a programmed event. We are preoccupied and fixated on church attendance, not only to measure church health but also to promote it to the masses as the way to deepen their faith. Not that we should de-emphasize going to church, but we must be clear that using attendance as a metric is not helping us, it's actually distracting us. Church attendance is measuring something; it's simply not measuring what we think it's measuring. It's producing a false positive.

Expanding and Growing the Church

The perspective of increasing the church's presence could take several forms. Perhaps the most common is the church growth perspective whose strategic goal is to expand an individual church and its programming. Another could be related to increasing the number of certain types of churches (replicating churches in a specific denomination or tradition) or creating more churches overall (church planting). In other words, build more impressive churches and build more of them. For the sake of discussion, I'll wrap these into the terminology of expanding the church's programming footprint.

Sustaining a church growth approach is contingent upon an ever-increasing number of people becoming involved in the systems of church. Typically, as newcomers get connected to a church they are encouraged to serve in some aspect of church programming (e.g., children's ministry, hospitality, worship, parking, etc.) and to donate money. The service hours and moneys are funneled into the church, which allows for expanded programming to make the church more attractive to new visitors. And with more visitors comes the need for bigger and more diverse physical space to conduct all the new programming and handle the bigger crowds. The additional visitors are also urged to play their part and help the church continue to grow, in order to reach more people and eventually start new campuses in other locations to continue the process.

> Using attendance as a metric is not helping us, it's actually distracting us. Church attendance is measuring something; it's simply not measuring what we think it's measuring. It's producing a false positive.

It's certainly impressive and marketable; the size and activity of a rapidly growing congregation creates a perception of vitality, progress, and excitement. But it is also singularly contingent on compelling new people into the system. If that falters or fails for any reason, like a leadership change or a crisis of any kind, the system cannot sustain itself and retraction occurs.

Beyond this is the issue of validity. This approach operates under two primary and mutually dependent assumptions. First, attending a growing church will transform a person's life and faith. And second, that the mission of the church is to increase its attendance and programming footprint.

The question not being asked is: Are those two assumptions valid? Let's explore each one.

Transforming Lives

The first assumption (that people attending a growing church will develop in their faith) was introduced in the previous section. As a learning and development practitioner, I can attest to a common and predominant fallacy: That attending an event will—on its own—lead to significant knowledge retention and behavior change.

It simply doesn't. Lasting knowledge, attitude and behavioral changes require targeted, accountable (and usually socially-integrated), behaviorally-based practices and processes. Development requires creating an awareness of the opportunity for change, identifying existing unhealthy practices and habits, introducing new knowledge and alternative behaviors, regular and consistent practice (ideally daily) with objective feedback to measure progress—all of which should be done in a context that allows for support and affirmation by others. You simply cannot include all these elements in an event like a church service and its associated programming.

21

The Church's Mission

The second assumption (that our mission is to increase the church's attendance and programming footprint) is obviously connected to the first. The church in the West views the gap between the annual net gain of 303 new church starts and the 3,205 needed to keep up with population (see the previous section) as the primary problem that must be solved. Armed with that statistic and motivated by a genuine desire to reach the lost in our communities, it's easy to assume the obvious solution is to start more and better churches. But if the footprint we've already established isn't making headway in transforming lives, what does growing that footprint accomplish?

The truth we must embrace in this conversation is that the mission given to us by Christ is not to increase the church's programming footprint, but instead to make disciples that intentionally follow Christ's teachings and commands.[10] Growing the church would make sense if church attendance and programming participation were developing people into effective disciples. But we've already seen this simply isn't the case.

Have we missionized the growth of church's footprint simply because we can; because it's expedient or expected? Would that mission change if our privileged status were to evaporate? And if the answer to that question is yes, why should it?

Think of it this way: If we focus on making disciples, we don't really have to be concerned about creating more church gatherings and events because they will occur naturally as a result. But if we continue with our current focus of creating more and better church gatherings, we very likely will not see more and better disciples made.

On another note, it is easy to lose sight of the reality that the church in the West—and particularly in North America—has been able to grow its visible presence because it enjoyed a privileged status for the entirety of its existence, in many ways even as far back as the Middle Ages. From tax privileges to the freedom from scrutiny, reprisal, or persecution, this privileged status is all we've ever known.

This privilege has been exposed recently when the COVID-19 stay-at-home social-distancing restrictions were instituted. I dare say no one saw in advance just how vulnerable the Western approach to church actually was. We have operated for centuries under the assumption that access to church programming was a given. Yet something as minuscule as a virus has thrown the viability of growing the church's footprint into serious doubt.

How has our privileged status (among other things) shaped what we see as our mission? In other words, have we missionized the growth of church's footprint simply because we can; because it's expedient or expected? Would that mission change if our privileged status were to evaporate?

And if the answer to that question is yes, why should it?

Have we become so fixated on growing the church's footprint that we fail to recognize it's not our true purpose? Are we satisfied with shooting for the wrong target, even if it's an admirable one?

Emphasis on Teaching and Knowledge

Teaching is a predominant ministry focus for most Protestant churches. In addition to the large congregational gatherings, these churches also typically provide mid-size groupings with a teaching emphasis for adults, students, and children. Even the mid-week small group structures in many churches center around Bible study as the primary activity. Consider also the volume of teaching and Bible education resources and programming consumed by the church in the West outside the local church setting.

The issue, of course, is not the usefulness or appropriateness of Bible education. After all, we are commanded and compelled to know and teach the Scriptures. The issue, instead, is one of balance.

Over-emphasizing Bible education comes with some cautions. For example, we must recognize that teaching is not training. As James commands, "Do not merely listen to the word, and so deceive yourselves. Do what it says" (Jas. 1:22). Teaching centers on cognitive understanding and factual retention. Training, on the other hand, moves beyond the cognitive domain to include the affective (feelings and values) and even the psychomotor (physical activity) domains by focusing on practical application and accountability around measurable behavior change and skill development (please see the Definition section for clarification on "accountability").

The most serious caution is that over-emphasis on education can produce knowledge without obedience (where obedience means following the leading of the Holy Spirit and observing the teachings of Jesus; it is not implying adherence to a legalistic, autocratic set of rules). Ultimately, this can foster a hypocritical, pharisaical attitude of pride that blocks the sanctifying work of God, demotivates us from living as Jesus lived and ruins our testimony. If we are serious about following Jesus, we must begin with the understanding that Jesus and the biblical authors consistently emphasize the priority of obedience to Jesus' commands. According to the Scriptures, obedience is both the ultimate expression of loving God and the true test of genuine faith in Christ.[11]

While educational programming elements have their place, they come with a cost. They disproportionately emphasize, model, incentivize, and reward knowledge and education, without providing the equivalent mechanisms to promote and support obedience.

This imbalance should concern us.

Disunity and Division

We give almost no thought to the vast number of denominations within Christianity in the West. We have split and differentiated ourselves over various doctrines, practices, traditions, ethnic and social values, polities, worship styles, methods of organization, theological viewpoints, and biblical interpretations. In the U.S. alone, there are over 300 separate denominations.[12]

The resulting effect is that we don't associate, practice, appreciate, collaborate, serve, or dialogue together beyond token measures. In fact, we take pride in our congregational distinctives and judge each other over them—sometimes harshly. Then, to make matters worse, we use these differences as marketing leverage to distinguish ourselves to prospective newcomers to our churches. This puts individual congregations in the curious position of competing with one another. New church starts often highlight their uniqueness compared to other churches, offering a "new experience" or a "fresh approach." Congregants of existing churches are attracted and end up church-hopping.

What would church look like if we were to include the church's unity in our prayer, "Your kingdom come, your will be done, on earth as it is in heaven"?

Have we ever stopped to ask ourselves how this reflects the biblical imperative to unity?

> "Make every effort to keep the unity of the Spirit through the bond of peace. There is one body and one Spirit, just as you were called to one hope when you were called; one Lord, one faith, one baptism; one God and Father of all" (Eph. 4:3–6).

How do our actions align with Jesus' hope for the church to be one— not just to tolerate one another but to have a oneness that resembles the unity of the Trinity itself?[13] Is our unity of sufficient quality to be unmistakable evidence to the lost that God exists? Is our unity serving as the great prerequisite to the whole world believing in God's love?

What does it say to a lost world when the many things dividing us are so much more important than the one thing that unites us? How do we calculate the ultimate cost of souls lost because of our choice to live disunified?

There are scriptural examples of Christians choosing to part ways from each other over strategy disagreement.[14] I fully grant that allowances for different viewpoints and practices can—and in many cases should—be made. But the wisdom comes in how we do it; in finding a way to be more practically and tangibly unified.

Admittedly, (not to overstate the obvious) unity is difficult to obtain. But we must also admit there's a flip side to this coin: Disunity is more convenient.

It is possible, if we come to agreement on our common mission; if we focus and prioritize the things we have in common and put our distinctives in the back seat. After all, unity will be our ultimate experience in the kingdom after our time here on earth is done. What would church look like if we were to include the church's unity in our prayer, "Your kingdom come, your will be done, on earth as it is in heaven"? How can and should we practically, tangibly, live this out? How do our current practices allow God to answer that prayer?

Organizational Dysfunction

Local churches are ripe for being poorly managed organizationally. Apart from the instances of serious misconduct and abuse on the part of high-profile church leaders, the broad (albeit largely anecdotal) evidence of widespread organizational dysfunction in the local church is difficult to dismiss.

You don't have to search too far to find a story about how churches managed their people, their finances, and their constituents using less-than-sound management practices. Rather than try to quantify levels of organizational dysfunction, I think it's more helpful to uncover the factors that lead to it.

The first thing to recognize is that organizational management is challenging. If it was easy, every business and non-profit would be healthy and sound. No human organization will be problem-free, so we need to be fair in approaching this conversation.

Churches, however, have some additional challenges to face. Though we position local church pastors as leaders, most have no background or training in the area of organizational management. Many pastors have little-to-no marketplace or practical experience to draw from, and have minimal understanding of management best practices.

Instead, pastors are trained in theology, philosophy, pastoral ministry (e.g., counseling), church history and Bible exegesis. Some seminaries and Bible colleges offer a few elective courses in leadership. Some even offer an alternative degree in leadership, but these typically amount to a handful of classes that provide only theory and conceptual understanding.

Pastors are then thrust into an executive organizational management role without the experience in how to do so. As a result, the organization often suffers from the lack of structures and procedures that produce organizational health in areas like financial management, administration, performance management, human resources, employment laws and practices, goal setting, strategy and planning, change management, learning and development, reporting, communication, conflict resolution, and accountability.

Smaller churches can suffer the most, because of insufficient funds to invest in organizational systems. Larger churches often will establish an executive pastoral role to focus on management issues, which is an improvement but not necessarily a guaranteed cure. Many denominations offer some administrative and executive leadership support, which is helpful, but this is often too far removed and too infrequent to provide the day-to-day, finger-on-the-pulse management that modern organizations require.

In my leadership coaching experience, I see this same pattern of organizational challenges in other specialty-service organizations like physician and legal practices. The organizations are typically small (ten staff members or less) and the recognized leaders are highly trained in the organizations' area of specialty—not in management. As a result, the leaders spend the bulk of their effort on practicing their specialty and not on running the organization. They also have little-to-no accountability or support (e.g., from a board of directors), so they have the freedom to run (or not run) the organization however they see fit. The leaders often are so elevated and esteemed for their specialty that it becomes difficult to challenge their authority, which usually leads to further dysfunction.

The result is we're asking pastors to perform a function they're not equipped for, in an organizational structure that provides limited mutual accountability and support. So churches suffer from being poorly-managed, which ultimately leads to ineffectiveness and reflects poorly on the gospel. This also complicates the strategy of trying to grow the church's footprint, since having more churches and more complex (i.e., larger) churches means we have proportionately fewer competent pastors to manage them.

The Biblical Picture of Church

We should consider that most of what we see in the modern church in the West isn't in the Bible. That's not to say the church's practices are unbiblical, but they are extra-biblical. Things like a senior pastor as an executive leader, buildings and church property, large weekly gatherings focused on preaching and worship, non-profit status, church membership status, voting for calling pastors and election of leadership ... these are all elements you don't see in the Scriptures.

To capture my point, try this exercise: Imagine yourself without any exposure to the modern North American church as we know it (CAWKI). This, of course, is a significant challenge for those whom the current approach to church is all they've ever seen. But try to limit your understanding only to the evidence in the Bible. Then take a natural reading of the New Testament and start a church based on what you've seen. This very likely will be difficult if CAWKI is all you've ever practiced. But if you can avoid the temptation of using today's church as the interpretation of "church," chances are what you come up with will not look like church as we know it today.

I readily concede that there is biblical evidence to support our current approach to church. I also concede the point that just because the components of CAWKI's ministry model aren't explicitly in the Bible doesn't make them wrong. "The internet isn't in the Bible," I've heard contemporary church leaders say, "but that doesn't mean we shouldn't use it to further the kingdom of God." Fair enough; I don't disagree.

But this perspective misses the point. It's not an issue of form, but rather one of function. There's a hard question we must ponder: How do these additional elements of the contemporary church impact its function? And to what degree do we maintain them unnecessarily, perhaps simply because we feel compelled to?

If we use the Scriptures as the model for church, then church as we know it now doesn't look like church as we see it then. Are you comfortable with the tension that creates, especially if we can also demonstrate that CAWKI is effectively blocking—however unintentionally—the spread of the gospel and the making of disciples?

29

It's Not ... But It Can

How would you respond if I told you that church as we know it in the West is not working? With indignation or insult? With resigned agreement but without hope for an alternative? Somewhere in between?

And if you disagree, what would you base it on?

And perhaps the most important question of all: If we can establish that our current approach to church is not working, are you comfortable with the consequences of continuing in that approach while untold millions of people miss out on the opportunity to become disciples of Jesus?

I encourage you not to react to the assertion that the church is not working. That assertion doesn't imply a lack of faithfulness or diligence. It doesn't question the church's motives or intentions, merely its effectiveness. I encourage you to instead to see it as an invitation.

> **If we can establish that our current approach to church is not working, are you comfortable with the consequences of continuing in that approach while untold millions of people miss out on the opportunity to become disciples of Jesus?**

The purpose of this chapter is to bring you to a point of pause, to create enough awareness that church as we know it may, in fact, not be working. This awareness will then position us to ask the truly important question, "What can we do?"

There is a better way that—up to now—we have failed to see or understand. It's an approach that...

- Turns every follower of Jesus Christ into an active disciplemaker and pushes the gospel outward into families, cultural niches, and social groups of all generations.

- Spans demographic and ethnic barriers to create a diverse expression of church that resembles the throng of people before the throne of God in the book of Revelation.
- Unifies the church, reaffirms the role of Jesus as the church's practical and functional Lord and Chief Servant, and de-emphasizes the beliefs, perspectives, and practices that keep us apart.
- Allows us—finally—to live out our individual and corporate calling to be the church Jesus died for.

This approach and the justification for it will be laid out in the chapters that follow. But before we discuss alternatives to CAWKI we must recognize the real challenge in embracing the new approach isn't based on information, it's our perception. CAWKI is normal for most of us in the West, so it is the starting point for evaluating "church"— and having so much invested in it makes it difficult to perceive the viability of any other approach.

The idea of perception is the next step in the process.

2 Paradigms and Perceptions

...one lives and analyses data within a frame, unaware that the solution is most often just outside of that frame. Never underestimate the depth of your subjectivity.

—Darrell Calkins

Offering a new way to view a well-established ministry model like the modern church is a risky endeavor. The perception of what church is and should be is strongly entrenched. It's deeply rooted socially and emotionally in both secular and religious communities—even people who don't go to church have a distinct mental picture of what they think it is. This perception is so accepted that it's difficult to objectively evaluate a new and different ministry model.

There is a strong prejudice for the existing model (and against anything that doesn't fit it). Any component of a new model—activities, priorities, perspectives, etc.—are all compared to the current model. If a new model doesn't align with or support the existing model it is viewed with skepticism, if not outright antagonism.

This paradigm exists in our mind because of certain patterns we have seen, which were then reinforced with experiences and the attitudes and emotions associated with those experiences. Once this paradigm is set, trying to see anything else is a challenge.

Paradigms Explained

The paradigm concept is not new, but in my experience its impact is often dismissed. I remember first learning of the concept of a paradigm when reading Steven Covey's classic *The Seven Habits of Highly Effective People.*[1] It was eye-opening for me at the time, and it connected so many dots on why change can be so difficult.

Covey illustrates the power of paradigms in recalling a group exer-cise from business school. The exercise involved using a version of the optical illusion image shown below, originally sketched by cartoonist William Ely Hill. If you're unfamiliar with Hill's sketch, you should examine it first to notice there are actually two women depicted: One is a beautiful young woman wearing a necklace and looking over her right shoulder, and the other is a profile view of an older woman with a prominent nose.

Covey's professor split the class into two groups. Each person received an image, but the two groups' images were slightly different versions of Hill's sketch. Group 1's version clearly emphasized the older woman, while Group 2's version emphasized the young and beautiful woman. He then showed the entire class a third image—the composite sketch showing both women.

After asking each group to describe what they saw in this final composite image, most said it was a variant of the first image they saw. In effect, the first image introduced a prejudice into each person's perspective: It biased their interpretation of the second similar image.

Once our brains evaluate a pattern and give it a definition they tend to default to it from then on, essentially locking in preferences to see only that pattern. It's one of the things that allows our brains to function efficiently, because they don't have to decipher or define the same pattern each time it's encountered. Unfortunately, it's also how two groups of people can look at the same thing and come away with virtually opposite interpretations!

This paradigm effect is deeply-seated in how we operate in the world around us. More recent studies on the same image were conducted using a broad age range of participants. When presented with the image for one-half second, the younger participants in the group claimed to recognize the young woman first and the older participants defaulted to seeing the older woman first, indicating the presence of a social bias on perception. In effect, participants' day-to-day social experiences biased their perception to focus on the elements in the image they were most familiar with.[2]

This highlights another bias effect to paradigms we must be aware of. Because the brain is such a capable pattern-recognition organ, it tends to favor the pattern it has already settled on and disfavor differing patterns. When you add significant social, emotional, or spiritual affinities onto this natural paradigm bias, the effect becomes even more solidified. The end result is that we project our preferred paradigm onto the world around us. This is the phenomena known as confirmation bias that impacts everything from legal eyewitness accounts to scientific study. Covey describes the impact:

"Each of us tends to think we see things as they are, that we are objective. But this is not the case. We see the world, not as *it is*, but as *we are*—or, as we are conditioned to see it. When we open our mouths to describe what we see, we in effect describe

35

ourselves, our perceptions, our paradigms. .... People see things differently, each looking through the unique lens of experience."[3]

Confirmation bias raises the stakes on the impact of paradigms. People don't easily give up on things they are dedicated to and have a significant investment in. They will resist changing it even when the new model can be defended and supported as a logically better alternative.

It's also important to understand that this process is amoral at

Because the brain is such a capable pattern-recognition organ, it tends to favor the pattern it has already settled on and disfavor any differing patterns.

its core: It's neither right nor wrong. The existence of paradigms, preconception of patterns, and biases toward one or more mental models are natural human phenomena and morally neutral processes. In the context of models of church form and structure, it's important not to assign any negative or judgmental connotation into the process or the use of terms like "bias." It simply means our brains have a natural preference and comfort level for what they've already seen and understood.

Paradigms and the Church

It's no understatement or exaggeration to say that church is a part of the personal identity for a great many Christians. They see much of their lives in the context of their church involvement, affinity, and membership. To suggest changing something they so strongly identify with is to threaten not just what they believe, but who they are.

The impact of a paradigm issue is precisely what Jesus spoke to when he was asked about his and his disciples' faith practices, which didn't align with accepted practices of the day. When questioned about why his disciples didn't regularly fast and pray, Jesus responded,

"No one tears a piece out of a new garment to patch an old one. Otherwise, they will have torn the new garment, and the patch from the new will not match the old. And no one pours new wine into old wineskins. Otherwise, the new wine will burst the skins; the wine will run out and the wineskins will be ruined. No, new wine must be poured into new wineskins. And no one after drinking old wine wants the new, for they say, 'The old is better'" (Luke 5:36–39).

I'm not suggesting that current legacy church practices are equivalent to the faith practices under the Mosaic code (the context for Jesus' illustration). I am, however, suggesting that the dynamics are very much the same for us today in considering a new and different model of church. Jesus and his disciples were practicing in a way that supported a different faith paradigm. The Pharisees, teachers of the law, and even the disciples of John the Baptist—the forerunner and precursor to the Messiah himself—operated from a different paradigm, one so different that it viewed Jesus' new practices as strange, confusing, and inappropriate.

The parable points out several keys about dealing with paradigm differences. First, the existing paradigm is outdated. The Greek word for "old" (*palaios*) in this passage carries the meaning of *obsoleteness*. It describes something that has existed for a long time, outlived its usefulness, been worn out by use, and is no longer valid or appropriate.

Second, the two paradigms are incompatible, so much so that mixing the two has significant implications. The old paradigm is well-established and inflexible. The new paradigm is still in the "fermentation" process, so it is transforming, expanding, and increasing in volume. Combining the two would both damage the old paradigm beyond repair and bring about the loss of the new paradigm in the process.

Third, people comfortable with the old paradigm will resist embracing the new when it is offered, preferring instead to stick with the old one. In my opinion, there are a variety of reasons for this choice, many of which I will address in later chapters. But it comes down to basic organizational and social change dynamics: Generally speaking, people resist changes that A) threaten valued practices or principles long-held as good or true, B) impact their habitual behaviors, or C) threaten their social status or position in a community. These dynamics reveal why change can be so difficult: There's a lot of inertia to overcome. All these dynamics work together to maintain the status quo. The motivation to change (dissatisfaction with the status quo) must be greater than the forces resisting the change.

The final and perhaps most obvious issue in dealing with the introduction of a new paradigm falls under the category of "if it ain't broke, don't fix it." If people are satisfied with the existing paradigm—even if they aren't fully vested in it—they simply won't be motivated to consider the new one. New paradigms require a lot of effort because there are new things to learn, new patterns to figure out. Virtually every step requires new decision-making processes because there are almost no precedents in place to guide them.

> Generally speaking, people resist changes that A) threaten valued practices or principles long-held as good or true, B) impact their habitual behaviors, or C) threaten their social status or position in a community.

This last dynamic has major implications when you're talking about the long-established paradigm of church in a Western society like the United States where even the secular view of church is well-entrenched. As discussed in chapter 1, many people consider themselves Christian simply by default; they aren't practicing any of the other known faith system like Judaism, Islam or Buddhism. They are Christian-ish; they don't consider themselves atheist or agnostic. They have enough familiarity with the current Christian paradigm to identify with it, even though they don't actively practice it. Yet even with such a casual adoption of Christianity they would still resist or question the validity of the new paradigm when confronted with it for the first time.

This makes it even more of a challenge for those who are devoted to and attend church regularly. In essence, it raises the stakes on considering a change to a new model of church that even the secular world would likely reject.

The Original

The final curiosity with the new church paradigm to be laid out in this book is that it is actually not new at all. In fact, it's ancient. It is a return to the original paradigm we see exhibited in the Gospels and the book of Acts. We can see it for what it truly was, if we look for a different image than the one we're used to.

To grasp the impact of this point, I invite you to take another look at William Ely Hill's sketch. Your brain will probably, once again, confirm the first image it identified, whether it was the old or the young woman. But each time you force yourself to see the opposite image—the one you were initially biased against—you'll see it quicker and with less effort. Eventually, you'll be able to identify both images with almost no effort at all.

My encouragement is to look at the image objectively, without allowing a natural bias or preference to prematurely and decisively connect the dots to your default paradigm. Because the corollary is also true: If you never try to see the other model, it will never come into focus for you.

If your preconception of church is the current legacy model of the church in the West, there is a different model of church than the one you're accustomed to. You can recognize this model if you give your-self permission to see it. The original model for church was what we now describe as a disciple-multiplying movement (DMM). It is an organic network of discipleship relationships, often organized around family units or existing relationship lines.

It was led at the outset by people authorized by Jesus himself (his disciples) and included the roughly 120 or so people who walked with him in his earthly ministry.[4] It grew rapidly through miracles and the movement of the Holy Spirit, spreading across the Roman Empire at the time even through extreme persecution. As more came to follow Jesus they joined the network and established churches with recognized groups of leaders. They typically met in homes, but they actively discipled others into surrendering their lives to Jesus and loving others into the community of faith.

> My encouragement is to look at the image objectively, without allowing a natural bias or preference to prematurely and decisively connect the dots to your default paradigm. Because the corollary is also true: If you never try to see the other model, it will never come into focus for you.

This model existed for nearly three centuries following the time of Jesus' resurrection. It is also currently being utilized in vibrant and growing churches and disciple-multiplying movements of the gospel around the world, where millions of people are coming to faith—often in conditions and circumstances mirroring the first-century church.

There's one more step we must take before considering the new DMM ministry model: We must understand how the practice of church changed from the generation following Jesus until today.

That's where we'll go next.

3   How Did We Get Here?

History, despite its wrenching pain, cannot be unlived, but if
faced with courage, need not be lived again.

—Maya Angelou

We must consider that the current Protestant ministry model has been in place for 500-plus years, and it was based on the Catholic church's model that existed many centuries before it. This long tenure has cemented our church model in place, giving it a nearly timeless perception. But actually, a number of internal and external forces have shaped the church in the West into what it is today. Understanding this formation will help us not only appreciate where we are, but also let us retrace our steps to Jesus' core message and practices.

And, well … it's history. So you'll probably find this chapter either fascinating or boring. If you're not a history buff, I encourage you to skip to the *Broad Observations of the History of CAWKI* section toward the end of this chapter. If you enjoy history, prepare yourself for a real discovery!

Church During the Roman Empire (c. 30 – c. 500)

Early Church Formation
Churches sprang up as believers fled Jerusalem to escape persecution. The new faith spread using the existing commercial, industrial, and

social connections. The Roman Empire provided a freedom of travel and interaction without hostile national barriers to cross.

Christians gathered together whenever and wherever they could. Through most of the second century this was in houses or low-key areas like cemeteries or catacombs. The seclusion allowed them privacy, and was a reflection of their poverty since they couldn't afford public meeting places.[1] This reclusive pattern contributed to a poor social perception of Christians who were thought to practice divination, incest, and even cannibalism.[2]

Christianity typically spread among the poor first, then gradually percolated up the social ranks as people in the middle- and upper-class began to believe. Slaves influenced slave owners, merchants influenced buyers, etc.[3] Even the Christian practice of caring for the sick (their own as well as those among the pagans) did much to change the perception of being a follower of Jesus. Not only did believers have a higher life expectancy, but the love displayed in serving others was evident. A notable example was the plague that hit the Roman Empire in the mid-200s. Christians in Carthage—blamed for the presence of the plague to begin with—could have adopted the pagan practice of abandoning their sick for fear of contamination. Instead they stayed to minister to the dying and to deal with the dead corpses piling up in the streets. Most of the believers died themselves in the process, but their dedication to love and serve their enemies won many converts.[4]

Ultimately, the message of the love of Christ and the Christian's devotion to and reverence of him trumped the decaying heathenistic belief system of the day.

The impact of individual believers' obedience in making disciples cannot be overstated. Schaff notes,

"It is a remarkable fact that after the days of the Apostles no names of great missionaries are mentioned till the opening of the middle ages ... There were no missionary societies, no missionary institutions, no organized efforts in the ante-Nicene age; and yet in less than 300 years from the death of St. John the whole population of the Roman empire which then represented the civilized world was nominally Christianized ... And while there were no professional missionaries devoting their whole life to this specific work, every congregation was a missionary society, and every Christian believer a missionary, inflamed by the love of Christ to convert his fellow-men."[5]

Ultimately, the message of the love of Christ and the Christian's devotion to and reverence of him trumped the decaying heathenistic belief system of the day. In the third century (especially the last half) the church experienced enormous growth as well as increased public tolerance and gradually started meeting more visibly in larger public buildings.

Persecution and Martyrdom
Even as the church grew through the first three centuries it faced seasons of extreme persecution. There were isolated accounts of official persecution in the first century (like Nero and Domitian) and again in the reign of Marcus Aurelius (161–180), but it became much more serious in the third century. The emperors Decius (250), Valerian (258), and Diocletian (303) each issued edicts for empire-wide persecution. The punishments included re-enslavement, purging the military of all Christians, banning public worship, destruction of church buildings, burning copies of the Scriptures, and execution for failure to participate in pagan sacrifices. Many recanted, but many others remained faithful. They went into hiding or were killed, including high-ranking church leaders and Senators—an indication that the faith had spread

even to the upper and ruling classes in Roman society by this time. Many Christians were even burned alive.

Generally speaking, the persecutions had a purifying effect on the church. Interestingly, the persecutions didn't slow the growth of Christianity. Whether it accelerated it, as Tertullian famously believed "The blood of the martyrs is the seed of the church,"[6] no one can be sure. The early believers' faithfulness is to be commended and—hopefully—imitated. During this roughly 300-year period, obeying Jesus' command to go and make disciples was a matter of conviction, not convenience.

Development of the Priesthood and the Bishopric
The apostles and early missionaries borrowed from pre-existing institutions to organize leadership. The English term of *bishop* (overseer, superintendent) has its origin in Greek communities, while the term *presbyter* (elder) has its roots in the Jewish synagogue. They are essentially the same function in the first-century church.

As the church in a given city grew, bishops/presbyters were identified to lead the bands of followers as a group. As decades passed, the model of civil authority structures began to influence the church and we see the emergence of individual leaders having authority over the others.

By the middle of the second century, bishops became the head of the collective churches in their cities. Presbyters came to refer to the council of shepherd-leaders that eventually formed the priesthood in the Catholic church, having pastoral oversight of individual congregations.

Gradually, bishops and priests assumed a sacerdotal authority, the mystical belief that they were sacred mediators between people and God. This eventually led to the practice that only priests could administer the sacraments like the Eucharist, confessions, baptisms, etc. By the fourth century, priests/presbyters were mandated, appointed congregational leaders, and by the Council at Carthage in 398, laymen were prohibited from teaching in the presence of clergy.[7]

By the end of the third century, bishops enjoyed a great amount of authority (and in a few cases abuses of power, wealth, and privilege). The bishops in the more prominent cities were most influential, chosen more from the higher social classes.[8] They were viewed as apostolic successors and even vicars (substitutes) of Christ himself. By the fourth century, the bishops of the major Roman political cities—Rome, Antioch, Alexandria and Constantinople (the new Rome)—came to have supreme jurisdiction and authority.[9] Eventually this settled on the bishops of Rome and Constantinople—the seeds of today's papacy of the Roman Catholic Church and the Ecumenical Patriarch of the Greek Orthodox Church.

Constantine, the First Christian Emperor

Constantine the Great, who reigned from 306–337, was the first Christian emperor. Though the maturity of his faith and the purity of his mission is debated, his influence on the church is without question. To have the emperor of Rome claim personal faith in Christ was a dramatic shift, and was previously considered unthinkable a century earlier by church historian Tertullian.[10]

His most significant impact came through the Edict of Milan (313) that granted Christianity legalized status. Once legalized and under Constantine's rule, the Christian values of mercy and justice began to influence the empire. Many cruel practices were discontinued or outlawed, including crucifixion, gladiatorial games, infanticide, and concubinage. The emancipation of slaves was encouraged and women's rights were greatly improved.[11]

The church grew in both size and reach as individual believers, through personal obedience to their calling, traveled into the nations and cultures as yet unreached by the gospel. There are accounts of unsponsored individuals who reached into Eastern Syria, Persia, Armenia, Georgia, Ethiopia, Scotland, and Ireland and to the Goths of Germania and Eastern Europe—many of the tribes that would later sack Rome had already heard of the gospel.[12] The church also grew in depth of theological and doctrinal insight. Much of the doctrinal foundation was laid in the fourth and early fifth centuries by such men as Athanasius, Ambrose, Augustine, Jerome, Chrysostom, Cyril, and Basil, who forged a trail of orthodoxy through a wilderness of heresy and heathenism.

But there were negative impacts as well. Large swaths of the population were baptized out of social and political expediency.

> "By taking in the whole population of the Roman empire the church became ... a church of the people, but at the same time more or less a church of the world. Christianity became a matter of fashion ... The line between church and world, between regenerate and unregenerate, between those who were Christians in name and those who were Christians in heart, was more or less obliterated, and in place of the former hostility between the two parties there came a fusion of them in the same outward communion of baptism and confession."[13]

The clergy became socially empowered, and what was previously a ministry of service became a new profession. Clergy enjoyed guaranteed income and exemption from military service. The church gained financial wealth it had never experienced previously, along with many privileges like tax-free status, legacies, and donations. At one point the church owned one-tenth of all landed property in the empire. The wealth (controlled by the bishops) was used to fund charitable services and ministries, but it also became a source for greed, indulgence, and financial abuse.

Constantine's efforts to mainstream the church into Roman society had impacts well after his death. Eventually, the Edict of Thessalonica (380) declared Christianity the official state religion. The church became integrated with the political and social structures throughout the empire. It was now legal—and fashionable—to be a practicing Christian. Many came into the church and were baptized not because they embraced the Savior, but because it was politically and socially expedient to do so. Such a rapid transition did not allow for the complete spiritual transformation of the heathenistic society. Philip Schaff summarizes this effect: "The christianizing of the state amounted therefore in great measure to a paganizing and secularizing of the church."[14]

The transition of status from persecuted to legalized to favored and finally to official in just sixty-seven years was embraced as "a reproduction of the theocratic constitution of the people of God under the ancient convent."[15] Constantine was the first in a string of emperors that ruled this presumed theocracy, where all the subjects are to be Christian. The state's civil and the church's religious rights are interconnected as "two arms of the same divine government on earth."[16]

The time of Constantine and the two centuries that followed was a hard right turn in the history of the church. The church gained political power, influence, and legal authority that rivaled the secular rulers.

> Constantine was the first in a string of emperors that ruled this presumed theocracy, where all the subjects are to be Christian. The state's civil and the church's religious rights are interconnected as "two arms of the same divine government on earth."

Being politically aligned and sponsored allowed for tremendous influence over public morals and religious practices, but also created an odd duality: public zeal for doctrinal purity mated with a private indifference to personal purity and morality. This had significant downstream effects, where political and social will of the empire—including the use of military might—were exercised under the banner of Christ.

This is a curious contrast to the actions and approach of Jesus, who shunned popularity, warned against abusing authority, avoided material wealth, seemed indifferent to political issues, and railed against a spiritual hypocrisy that judged others at the exclusion of holiness and righteousness.

Some of the greatest theological minds in church history (Ambrose, Chrysostom, Basil, Jerome, and Augustine) contributed to significant doctrinal refinement of major doctrinal issues that had divided the church for centuries.[17] Yet at the same time, the quality of the priesthood degraded as many unqualified men were attracted to the wealth and influence of the church. From the middle of the fifth century on, it was rare to find any clergy who knew the original languages of the Scriptures.[18]

The Medieval Church (c. 500 – c. 1500)

After Constantine, the church inherited the responsibility for education and sponsorship of the arts and sciences, which it was ill-prepared for. Facing a general social and philosophical decay and the constant threat of barbarian invasion, the church in the West moved away from Greek influence and became decidedly Latin.

This period begins with the social aftermath of the fall of Rome and the last Western Roman emperor in 476. The church became the stabilizing factor in Western Europe, setting the stage for what would eventually result in feudalism as a social structure. This was the context for the formalization of hierarchical papal leadership, especially under Gregory the Great (590–604).[19]

The emphasis of the priesthood of all believers diminished and the divide between the laity and clergy increased. The ordination process for the priesthood was formalized and celibacy developed into a common practice. The process of electing bishops by popular vote became increasingly political and corrupted. By the eighth century in the East and the eleventh century in the West, bishops were chosen by the vote of the other bishops or were appointed by the secular ruler.

Liturgies, elements, and practices of church gatherings developed in the fourth to the sixth centuries were now codified and standardized in the sixth to the seventh centuries. They became more elaborate for a number of reasons: to bring order and uniformity to practice of worship, to accommodate unlearned bishops and priests, to maintain the appearance of connection to the apostolic foundations of the church, and to prevent heretical influences and changes from finding their way into the worship.[20]

With all the changes both inside and outside the church, it is remarkable that Christianity continued to have influence over not only the Roman Empire but also over the barbarians who threatened and finally succeeded in overthrowing the empire. The efforts of the early missionaries to the tribes of Europe brought language, science, and a brotherhood society, though it was a superficial faith centered more on church tradition than apostolic belief in Jesus.[21]

Monasticism

The fervor of monasticism was a response to the increasing secularization of the church. In the first few centuries it was actually a rejection of the church.[22] It eventually became a rival of the priesthood, a separate order somewhere between priests and laity. Monks took upon themselves voluntary practices of celibacy, poverty, absolute obedience, and often excessive self-punishment in the effort to achieve personal holiness.[23] Monks and the ascetic life they lived were popular and admired, so much so that they created an odd barrier—as if personal holiness for the common believer was unattainable and inferior.[24]

Though it began in the third century and exploded in the fourth and fifth, its greatest influence came in the Middle Ages. Monasteries became one of the few places where structured education was available.[25] Eventually monks became actively involved in the mission of the church, and a monk actually became one of the church's most influential popes: Gregory the Great.

The Spread of Islam

The Islamic expansion came out of Arabia in the last half of the seventh century into what is now the Middle East, overtaking the formerly Christian centers of Jerusalem, Antioch, and Alexandria, then Babylon, Armenia and Georgia. North Africa was conquered, and by 709 Christianity had disappeared altogether in North Africa.[26]

Nominalism of the church in the East was part of the drought that fed the wildfire growth of Islam. Much of the church in these regions had long since become superficially Christian, with heretical beliefs in the deity of Jesus and mixing Christian practices with paganism. Some areas actually viewed their conquerors as liberators from the Eastern Roman emperor's rule.[27]

Islam's expansion from Africa through Spain was eventually stopped in Tours (France) in 732 by the armies of Charles Martel—a leader of the Franks, whom the Catholic Church had aligned with politically after the fall of Rome.

The Holy Roman Empire

After the decay and fall of political Rome, the church leveraged its missionary efforts among the barbarians into a string of political relationships throughout Western Europe. It allied itself with a series of military leaders that culminated in the Carolingian dynasty and Charlemagne, whose rule included the majority of Western and Central Europe. Inspired by Augustine's *City of God* (which he had read to him every night), he enforced submission to Christianity through military conquest. In 800, he was crowned "Emperor of the Romans" by Pope Leo III, thus initiating the Holy Roman Empire.

This part of church history is nearly unmatched in the church's political and social power. The political rule of the new empire and the religious and social authority of the church were symbiotic. The church managed much of the lands and social life of the empire in a feudal arrangement and the empire provided both protection and expansion of the church through military conquest and rule.[28] This set the stage for the later crusades (1095–1271) in which the church offered military service as a penance. The combined motifs of pilgrimage to Jerusalem and authorized, pious violence seen in the crusades sound eerily like the theme of jihad used by radical Islamic groups today.[29]

The empire itself existed formally from 800–1806, surviving Viking invasions from the Scandinavians in the North and a number of transitions of power from Carolingian dynasty to a decentralized mix of rulers, lords, principalities, etc., until the empire dissolved in the Napoleonic Wars. The church was marred by papal moral decay (though there were some exceptions), and a general lack of missionary spiritual focus.

East-West Divide

During this period a growing animosity developed between the Papal authority of the Western Church and the leader of the church in the east, the Ecumenical Patriarch. Although the two churches shared much in terms of doctrine, theology, and dogma, the cultural differences and political alignments drove the seeds of division deep. The two offices became a political and theological rivalry that would last for some 600 years.

After the Western empire fell, the church in Rome was forced to engage in the social events of medieval Western Europe. However, it was still technically under the political dominion of the Eastern emperor who expected Rome to obey. This situation made for an awkward dependency for the church in the West, which increasingly found itself aspiring to increasing its power and influence.[30]

The Eastern church's identity centered on the local assembly united in eucharistic fellowship and the celebration of the sacraments. In contrast, the church in Rome operated more from the emphasis of canonical law and submission to a monarchic head. When added to the political alliances and the struggle for authority and control, the differences ultimately culminated in the leaders excommunicating each other in 1054. The churches split, creating what are now the Roman Catholic and Greek Orthodox denominations.

Prior to scholasticism, philosophy and theology was the study of the practical discipline of virtuous living and the admiration of the divine. After scholasticism they became theoretical disciplines involving dialectical debate, metaphysics, and speculation.

The specific grievances and differences of opinion between the churches are varied, ranging from disagreements over ultimate authority to such trivial issues as the type of bread used in the Eucharist (leavened vs. unleavened), to clergy celibacy, to how many days after birth a child should be baptized. At its core the real issue was, as Ferguson notes, "the loss of the will to unity."[31]

After the split the church in the East existed for a time without significant change. It was able to make inroads into the Slavic tribes of Eastern Europe and the Russian empire, but beyond that made no serious missionary advances. According to Schaff, "In doctrine, worship, and organization, she stopped at the position of the œcumenical councils and the patriarchal constitution of the fifth century."[32] It was significantly weakened by the growth of the Ottoman Empire which eventually overthrew Constantinople in 1453.

Scholasticism
Scholasticism was an intellectual revival from the twelfth to fourteenth centuries that moved education beyond the monasteries to a broader audience. It started in cathedrals then gradually grew into independent centers led by specific influential teachers and philosophers. Scholasticism initiated a transition from oral learning based upon the moral authority of the teacher to one based on logic, philosophy, and reasoning of written texts. Prior to scholasticism, philosophy and theology was the study of the practical discipline of virtuous living and the admiration of the divine. After scholasticism they became theoretical disciplines involving dialectical debate, metaphysics, and speculation.[33]

On the positive side, Scholasticism contributed to the formation of systematic theologies and *lectio*, a method of teaching involving reading of a text followed by a lecture on a commentary of the text's meaning. Yet it also produced many of the dogmatic medieval practices of the Catholic Church, like limiting communion for the laity and creating the treasury of merit, the basis for the sale of indulgences.[34] Scholasticism in the church set the example for higher education on a broader, secular level, with the creation of the first universities in Europe.[35]

Later Medieval Decay

The later medieval period saw a general decay in the church in the West that had become increasingly authoritarian. The few serious attempts at reform failed as by now the church had too much political inertia to overcome. "Heresy" was broadened from doctrinal deviance to include a perceived lack of submission to authority. This was the slippery slope that created the Inquisitions.

The church in this period is marked by a lack of evangelism, pastoral care, and teaching. Priests widely practiced concubinage. At times multiple popes claimed their authority. Participation in church gatherings became obligatory and ritualistic as the church prioritized confession and duty. The mass—conducted in Latin, which by now only a minority of people spoke—increasingly became a "ritual celebrated for the people rather than with the people."[36]

The Renaissance Church (c. 1300 – c. 1700)

The church in this time period cannot be rightly understood apart from the Renaissance, which saw the rise of humanism, "The genius of man ... the unique and extraordinary ability of the human mind."[37] Coincidentally, the Renaissance was inspired by the influx of Greek teaching, philosophy, and literature that fled Constantinople when it was overthrown in 1453.[38] The Renaissance brought an avalanche of change, including the printing press, discovery of the Americas, a revival of classic literature and Greek philosophy, the development of diplomacy, observation and inductive reasoning, the beginnings of national identity and independence, and the growing passion for individual intellectual and spiritual freedom. These are juxtaposed to a static, decaying, self-serving papal theocracy.[39] In this setting it was only a matter of time before reform became not just an opportunity, but an identity; a way of life that has shaped church operation ever since.

The Reformation

The Reformation didn't begin with Luther's nailing the *NinetyFive Theses* on the door of the Wittenburg Cathedral in 1517, though it's probably its most iconic event. The Reformation was a broad response to the Catholic Church's abuse of power and self-serving, corrupt authority. The most prevalent abuse was the papal sale of indulgences, but there were many others. Many people preceded Luther as skeptics and outspoken critics (Valla, Wycliffe, Hus, von Goch, von Wesel, Wessel, Wyttenbach, et al.).[40]

It's important to understand that the Renaissance was the framework for the Reformation: Humanism was the mindset for most of the reformers, both inside and outside Catholicism (Erasmus, Zwingli, Thomas More, Luther, and Calvin). It was (ironically and in part) a reaction to the church's education that had banned the study of the classic authors and institutions.[41] The Protestant Reformation was "a protest against human authority, assert[ing] the right of private conscience and judgment, and rous[ing] a spirit of criticism and free inquiry."[42] Without the Renaissance, the Reformation never happens.[43]

> The Protestant Reformation was "a protest against human authority, asserting the right of private conscience and judgment, and rousing a spirit of criticism and free inquiry." Without the Renaissance, the Reformation never happens.

Out of the Reformation come the well-known tenets of the authority of Scripture and individual faith in Christ. But we also see the practical impacts on church practices. In worship, for example, the sermon receives a prominent focus, along with the restoration of celebrating congregational communion and speaking the local language instead of Latin. Thousands of hymns are attributed to the Reformation period. We also see an increased emphasis on catechetical instruction and schools established for educating the common people. The Reformation also elevated the laity and the priesthood of the believer, though the ordination of clergy authorized to conduct the sacraments remained.[44] The Reformation had a response within the Catholic Church as well in the form of the Counter-Reformation that corrected many of the abuses and shortcomings of the church's leadership. The Reformation was as much a social reality as it was a theological or ecclesiastical one.

Widespread persecution broke out across Europe as the Catholic Church reacted to it. On the other side, the German Reformation gave authority to the civil authorities to oversee the church in lieu of papal authority. This led to state-sponsored persecution (inspired by the Reformers) of the Catholics who didn't align with Reformation practices.[45] It all led to conflicts like the Thirty-Years War (1618–1648), fought between various Protestant and Catholic states within the Holy Roman Empire and resulted in eight million fatalities. Most of Europe was involved, but Germany was particularly hard hit: An estimated 20 percent of the population of Germany died.[46]

The Modern Church (c. 1700 – present)

The modern church in the West was born in the Enlightenment, the evolution of the Renaissance. The Enlightenment was an elevation of thought and philosophy, where reason and empiricism (empirical evidence gained through the senses) became the primary source of knowledge. It advanced the ideals of liberty, progress, toleration, fraternity, constitutional government and separation of church and state, scientific method, and reductionism. As a result, rebellion against authority (both monarchical and ecclesiastical), fixed dogmas, and religious orthodoxy were common Enlightenment expressions.

Denominationalism

The spirit of individualism that bore the Reformation continued in creating a wave of denominationalism. The Reformation was not a unified response to Catholic theology, but rather a splintered one that produced separate groups aligned with the primary reformers (initially Luther, Zwingli, Calvin, and the Anabaptists). It quickly spread to disparate groups—all of whom shared an odd allegiance of opposition to the Catholic Church while also (with varying severity) opposing each other. At the core of it all was the opportunity, privilege, and drive of religious liberty and autonomy:

"The tendency of Protestantism towards individualism did not stop with the . . . Reformation churches, but produced other divisions where it was left free to formulate and organize the differences of theological parties and schools."[47]

This sense of individual autonomy produced a flurry of denominations in the eighteenth and nineteenth centuries, including Episcopalian, Lutheran, Presbyterian, Congregationalist, Methodist, and Baptists. Once many of these denominations spread to America—where there was no government to interfere or restrict their actions—they blossomed into the many varied groupings we see today.[48]

Evangelicalism and The Great Awakenings

The development of evangelicalism came from the increased focus on individual faith—contrasting sharply with faith required by the established, tax-supported and state-sponsored church. The

Enlightenment value of individualism continued to flourish and evolve into an emphasis on personal faith experience.

The American war of independence from Britain highlighted this even more, creating a fertile environment for its growth. This became evident particularly in the middle American colonies, which were fast-growing, prosperous, and socially and ecclesiastically diverse. The population was rapidly increasing in both England and America, and the existing church structures could not meet the demand for individual pastoral care. The need for—and the perceived value of—a state-sponsored church simply evaporated. Hence, the American Constitution in 1789 prohibited the federal government from favoring a particular denomination.[49]

The spirit of individualism that bore the Reformation continued in creating a wave of denominationalism.

Into this opportunity stepped the likes of George Whitefield, John and Charles Wesley, and Jonathan Edwards, who recognized the signs of the times and the movement of the Spirit. They fervently preached both in churches and outdoor gatherings (at the time an unorthodox and indecent departure from high church practices) on the gospel and the individual response to it, leading to the emphasis on a personal salvation.

The approach sparked a series of spiritual revivals both in America and in Great Britain called the Great Awakenings. The first began in the mid-1700s, followed by another in the late 1790s to the middle of the nineteenth century and a third from the latter half of the nineteenth century into the 1930s. These movements were also associated with a deliberate and well-documented emphases on extraordinary prayer.[50]

The results of the Awakenings are debated, but there are some notable high-level outcomes. First, the Awakenings defined evangelicalism as a cross-denominational social segment (especially in the U.S.). Second, large numbers of blacks came to faith and many of the primarily African-American denominations we see today were started. When combined with the social reality of slavery and the Civil War, there is a practical divide between white and black Christians in America that persists today. Third, the emphasis on the supernatural spurred the growth of the charismatic movement and development of charismatic theology.[51] Finally, and perhaps most profound, the Awakenings individualized faith at a personal, experiential level and tied it to contemporary social issues. This created the language and practice of revival, and influenced everything from denominational emphases, to social organizations (e.g., the YMCA), to faith-based responses to social issues like slavery, temperance, and women's rights.[52]

> The Awakenings individualized faith at a personal, experiential level and tied it to contemporary social issues. This created the language and practice of revival...

The Awakenings set up church as we know it in America today. The outcomes observed above have continued to develop in the way church is practiced, particularly in the gradual departure from an institutional or traditional identity and the rise in popularity of the non-denominational churches. We've seen it in the Jesus People movement in the late '60s and '70s. It fostered the seeker-sensitive approach and postmodern emphasis in the '80s and '90s (perhaps the most notable example being Willow Creek Community Church in South Barrington, Illinois). It produced the now widely-practiced attractional church growth strategy of planting and growing churches that appeal to those disassociated from church.

Broad Observations of the History of CAWKI

Stepping back from the flow of church history to see the entire picture reveals certain themes that are relevant in comparing CAWKI and DMM.

The Kingdom Impact of Individual Believers

The gospel spread through normal people being obedient to Jesus commands to go, make disciples, and love and serve one another. Especially before but even after hierarchical and government-sponsored church leadership was established, the expansion of the gospel has consistently come as a result of the obedience of individual believers responding in faith and obeying Christ's commands.

The Church and the State

Becoming the state-sponsored religion did little to help the disciple-making mission, and one could argue it did much to diffuse it. If everyone is already a "Christian," then from what do they repent? And why would someone surrender their life to Christ? The pattern of christianizing the general population of Rome remains a residual cultural reality in the West—particularly in the U.S., where we often wrestle with the concept of being a "Christian nation"—something the church in most of the rest of the world does not experience.

In all fairness to the church in Rome in AD 313: If I'd lived during this time of empire-sponsored persecution, I would likely have seen Constantine's conversion and granting legal status to the church as God-ordained deliverance and authorization. It would have been difficult to reject the privilege and political power, and instead maintain a humble focus on loving God and loving people. We should consider that history seems to confirm two things that must be held in tension: 1) it *was* God's deliverance, and 2) it *was not* a divine call to create a Christian empire.

So how do we best carry out the commands of Christ in a democratic society of religious freedom and prosperity with Jesus as our only sovereign over a kingdom that supersedes this world? It is indeed an important question. The temptation to seize and leverage political power is difficult to resist in any era. How the U.S. church relates with our social and political spheres is critical; we should tread wisely and carefully, recognizing there are (both good and bad) lessons to be learned from the early Roman church's embrace of a theocracy. Above all, it would seem wise to follow Jesus' lead and "render to Caesar the things that are Caesar's, and to God the things that are God's" (Matt. 12:17).

Monasticism

The rise of monasticism did much to pull the Western Roman church back to spiritual purity, personal holiness, and devotion to Christ. On the other hand, monasticism had many questionable practices and perspectives that border on the extreme of fanatical asceticism for asceticism's sake. The drive for things like isolation, silence, and mystical experiences are a curious contrast to Jesus' call to go and make disciples and engage with sinners in a fallen world.

The pattern of christianizing the general population of Rome remains a residual cultural reality in the West— particularly in the U.S., where we often wrestle with the concept of being a "Christian nation."

The laity's esteem and veneration of a monk's lifestyle only cemented the perception that true spirituality is reserved for a special class of believers. One has to wonder: If the church had maintained its early and fierce devotion to Christ's commands to love God and neighbor and to make disciples of all nations—instead of becoming so secularized—would monasticism ever have come about as it did? And how does monasticism's pursuit of the uber-spiritual experience impact our practice of making disciples?

Church Leadership and Laity

Church leadership in the West organized itself using the pattern of the social and political structures of the Roman Empire. It was an easy evolution for the bishops in the major cities to begin governing the rest of the church and to give authority to the priests. Combined with the development of the sacerdotal priesthood, it's no surprise that a new classification of believers was created: The laity.

Most Westerners claiming to know Christ today are in this category, reporting to the authority of the designated pastor/teacher. Church meetings follow this pattern of the congregation sitting as an audience, observing the elevated role of the priest—and after the Reformation the senior minister—conducting the service. The call of the laity to participate in the functions of the church and the Great Commission are marginalized and de-emphasized.

> Division—while painful and unpleasant— is simply more convenient than unity.

Division

The unsightly reality of division started fairly early and has been a regular theme in the church's history. Divisions were exacerbated by the church's relationship with the state, which created an awkward response: Conform or lose privilege and face excommunication—if not execution.

Two divides stand out the most: the Great Schism in 1054 and the Protestant Reformation that set the stage for a wave of denomination-alist fervor that followed. I'll take a deeper look at the importance of unity and its impact on our mission in chapter 5 (specifically, *Contrast #3 – Organizing Principle: Differentiation vs. Unity* [page 93]). But in reflecting on the history of the church, the lack of unity has clearly left its mark.

Perhaps the most sobering observation is division has often been a consequence of ineffective leadership. When leadership disregards humility, integrity, servanthood and love, it becomes privileged, worldly, ineffective, authoritarian, and self-serving. This is the soil where the seeds of division take root.

We would do well to take a full accounting of our history of division, and be mindful of not only the negative impacts to our fellowship but (more importantly) the example we set for the people we are called to serve. Division—while painful and unpleasant—is simply more convenient than unity.

Renaissance and Enlightenment Thinking

The Renaissance brought many positive things to Western Europe as it came out of the Middle Ages. This period advanced many aspects of European society, from education to scientific study and innovation. In a sense, it was the sapling that has matured some 300 years later into the Information Age. The Gutenberg Press made information and learning available to the masses, much as the internet in our age has provided universal, on-demand access to information to anyone with a smart phone.

The Renaissance's elevation of knowledge (in part) fueled the Reformation, which in turn shaped the Enlightenment. The Renaissance and the Enlightenment together had the tectonic effect of shaping the church's priorities of teaching and promoting an intellectually-based faith.

Emphasis on Evangelism

The drive for evangelism and a personal faith conversion to Christ became the pre-eminent mission of the Protestant church coming out of the Great Awakenings, and became the signature identity of much of the church in the West. Today we continue to emphasize the priority of personal salvation as the ultimate goal of the Christian life.

The emphasis was undoubtedly appropriate and beneficial from a historical perspective. That said, what legacy has it left the church in the West when it comes to disciple-making? What if the itinerant evangelists during the Awakenings had not stopped at the message of the gospel for the individual, and had instead gone on to include the empowering message of being a disciple-making disciple? I'll address parts of this question in chapter 6 (*Contrast #6 – Ministry Goal: Salvations vs. Disciple-Makers* [page 106]).

What if the itinerant evangelists during the Awakenings had not stopped at the message of the gospel for the individual, and had instead gone on to include the empowering message of being a disciple-making disciple?

We Are, In Part, What We've Become

It's easy to disregard how the two millennia of societal forces and reactions have shaped the church's methods and priorities. Said a different way: We think we're painting the portrait of our faith practices on a blank canvas, but in reality we're painting over the practices of those who've preceded us—and their portraits are mixing into ours. The discipline comes in looking back to the original as a point of reference: The longer history progresses, the further back we have to look.

As a case in point, compare the socio-religious dynamics in the first century with today (particularly the U.S.). The early church faced the enormously challenging question of how to incorporate Jews, Samaritans, and Gentiles into the church. At the time of Christ, these three groups were separated by chasms of ethnic, social, and religious differences. They took the approach that Jesus modeled, believing that belief in Christ and unconditional love made everyone equal. As Paul wrote:

"There is neither Jew nor Gentile, neither slave nor free, nor is there male and female, for you are all one in Christ Jesus. If you belong to Christ, then you are Abraham's seed, and heirs according to the promise. ... Here there is no Gentile or Jew, circumcised or uncircumcised, barbarian, Scythian, slave or free, but Christ is all, and is in all" (Gal. 3:28-29, Col. 3:11).

Fast forward to America in the 1600-1700s, when Christianity spread to the African slaves and the black community during the Great Awakenings. By this time, the church was deep into its denominational fervor. Autonomy and separating over differences, both a legacy of the Reformation, were normal practices. The church was distracted and missed the Bible's admonition for unity.

There were a few calls for racial equality, social unity, and even the abolition of slavery. But they were lost in the noise of independence from England and the economics of slavery in the South. When large numbers of blacks came to faith, the attitudes of autonomy and separation predominated and they weren't treated as equals. In turn, black believers formed their own denominations.

I grant that this is a complex issue, and oversimplification—along with a hefty dose of 20/20 hindsight—makes it tempting to paint with a broad brush. My point is simply that the church missed an opportunity to set a social example for unity. Its missional focus and priority of love was lost in the myopia of independence and separation. Now, more than 200 years later, we're still wrestling with the social aftermath of racial division and misunderstanding stemming from this missed opportunity.

"I Will Build My Church"

The most obvious—and encouraging—historical observation is the resiliency of the church, despite all it's faced in its tumultuous history. The church has endured everything from the annihilation of persecution to the temptations of privilege, political alignment, secularization, and everything in between. In his sovereign partnership with us, God has allowed us to make choices that have shaped the church throughout its history—in both beneficial and counterproductive ways. Still, God has always raised up champions of the faith and opened doors of opportunity that faithful believers walked through. The love of Christ has continued to work in the hearts of his people. Jesus' prediction of the gates of hell not overcoming the church has been proven true, and history gives us the confidence to believe it will continue to be true until he returns to claim his bride.

4 Multiplication: What and Why

People don't buy what you do, they buy why you do it. And what you do simply proves what you believe.

—Simon Sinek

Now that we see the full scope of how CAWKI came to be, we are in a position to investigate the concept of multiplication and its role in church strategy. Multiplication is the process by which Christianity spread from Judea through the Roman Empire in roughly 300 years. As we've seen, most of this movement occurred through the grassroots effort of individual people. The act of calling others to a transformed life in Christ was embedded into the common, individual believers' faith practice—and the world simply couldn't resist it. It's what's been lost in CAWKI, and it represents the single-greatest opportunity for kingdom impact awaiting the legacy church in the West today.

Multiplication drives disciple-multiplying movements: Without multiplication it is impossible to create and sustain a movement. Multiplication is the key to accomplishing the Great Commission: reaching large numbers of individuals, families, groups, and sub-cultures, and eventually whole communities, regions and ethnic groups. It infuses and contextualizes the gospel into a group's culture, ultimately transforming it from the inside out as significant numbers of people in the group come to faith and re-orient their lives around being a disciple of Jesus.

Multiplication: The What

Multiplication is the outcome of people sharing their life in Christ with others early (i.e., in their faith journey) and often. People will eventually respond with interest, and when they do the follower of Christ personally begins to disciple them. This, Lord willing, eventually leads the person being discipled to believe in Jesus. Along the way, the disciple-maker equips the person being discipled to share their faith experience with others—implementing the disciple-making process modeled for them.

Once the person being discipled (the second-generation disciple) begins to disciple others, the first-generation disciple continues to mentor and stay connected with the second-generation disciple to assist and provide wisdom and counsel as needed. But the first-generation disciple is also freed up to disciple the next person who shows an interest and responds to the gospel.

Multiplication occurs as this process is repeated over time. One disciple becomes two, two becomes four, four becomes eight, eight becomes sixteen ... where each successive generation doubles the number of the previous generation.

Along the way, groups of these disciples meet regularly as a community to practice all the "one-anothers" (love one another, encourage one another, serve one another, etc.). These groups gather, ideally weekly, anywhere they want: homes, businesses, parks, etc. Most of these groups will eventually deepen in their commitment to the Lord and to each other to conduct the functions of church described in the New Testament: worship, prayer, Bible study, fellowship, support, encouragement, accountability, celebrating Communion, baptizing new believers, giving, etc.

Each disciple in the network is encouraged and equipped to be a part of two groups: one that serves as their primary spiritual family (a "home church") and another that is led by a person they are discipling. In this way disciples are always "going" to engage other people in discipleship and introducing the gospel into the relationship networks of the person being discipled.

The leaders of these groups assume responsibility for overseeing all the discipleship practices in a worthy and appropriate manner, and remain connected and accountable to the person who has discipled them. Because these mentoring relationships are maintained, the groups become connected in a network of groups that share resources and support each other, interacting at a group level across neighborhoods, the city, and the region. As the number of disciples and groups increases, more seasoned and mature leaders take on the role of overseeing and managing the conduct, spiritual health, and progress of the groups.

> Multiplication is the key to accomplishing the Great Commission: reaching large numbers of individuals, families, groups, and sub-cultures, and eventually whole communities, regions and ethnic groups.

Over time, the entire process scales in every area until the groups represent a city church with sufficient reach and resources to begin transforming the communities in which they reside. Rather than being identified as a building or a location, the church is identified as the collection of disciples in the network. These disciples are free to gather at every level for their various activities: two or three, eight to twelve, thirty to fifty and above. The church is the followers of Christ collectively living out their faith and following the commands of Jesus.

Frequency and Rapidity
An analogy to discipleship multiplication is the concept of "going viral," a process where an image, video, meme, etc., gets shared frequently between people via social media. It usually reaches viral status based on two things:

1. How *often* it is shared (e.g., over half of the videos on YouTube have less than 500 views, while those considered viral—fewer than one percent of videos—have more than 1 million views).
2. How *quickly* it is shared (e.g., 40,000 hits in one hour).

Discipleship movements are, of course, different from merely sharing a video on social media; after all, popularity is not the driving force behind discipleship. Discipleship movements are people responding to the call of God to both *be* a disciple and then to *make* disciples—or even more technically accurate, to make disciple-*makers*. But in comparison to Western church growth patterns and processes, multiplication does have the similar qualities of being shared often and quickly. For clarity's sake, I'll label these as frequency and rapidity.

Frequency

The impact of frequency comes when believers share the gospel and their faith story often and widely. Many people will not respond to this sharing, but some—those who deeply desire to be a part of the kingdom of God—eventually will. The goal is to find the people who are truly searching and hungry to know God, not just those who are curious or casually interested.

Rapidity

Once someone does respond, the focus of the disciple-maker shifts from sharing with many to investing deeply in the few who respond by mentoring and modeling the core practices of the Christian faith. This is where the impact of rapidity comes into play. The mentor disciple encourages and equips the new disciple to begin sharing the gospel (relatively) quickly. And the disciple-making process begins with another generation.

In truth, the believers sharing their faith need only be a few faith steps ahead of the person they are discipling. Sometimes the sharing of faith happens even before the point of conversion. The person sharing reveals what she knows without being limited by what she doesn't know. Her own faith and knowledge increase rapidly as she comes to faith. Her mentor disciple continues to pour into her and provides teaching, knowledge, support, and accountability. Deeper doctrinal or theological questions that can't be answered are escalated up the mentoring/discipleship chain of relationships to someone who is sufficiently knowledgeable and equipped to teach. Once addressed, the new disciple continues to grow on her faith journey.

An Example

As an example, let's say a new believer, Tom, has put his faith in Christ only two months ago through the influence of his co-worker Eric. Eric encourages Tom to begin praying for God to reveal to whom he should share the good news of his new faith. In prayer he is reminded of Frank, his neighbor three doors down with whom he occasionally invites over to have a beer and watch a game. Following the Spirit's promptings, Tom shares his story of how he was introduced to Christ, his understanding of the significance of being saved from sin and the joy of having new life and the Holy Spirit living inside him.

Frank is curious, but skeptical. After all, this was out of blue: He and Tom have never talked about spiritual matters before—it's always been about sports and the frustrations of their jobs. But Frank has a gut feeling Tom may be on to something. Tom's always been a normal guy in the three years they've known each other, so for him to talk about this so openly and plainly impresses Frank. He senses Tom's commitment and convictions are genuine. And on a deeper level, Tom's newfound hope and conviction make Frank keenly aware of his own hopelessness. Could this Jesus stuff be real after all, and could it be the solution to his own emptiness?

With some apprehension, Frank shares his thoughts with his wife, Sue. Sue is taken aback—she's only heard Frank talk about religion a handful of times in their seven-year marriage, and those were always critical. But she sees this is different. The fact that Frank would share something this personal speaks volumes, given the lack of intimacy that has crept into their marriage over the last several years. Though a bit afraid of where all this might be going, she surprises herself by suggesting that they have Tom and his wife over for dinner to talk more about it.

The Keys to Frequent and Rapid Sharing of Faith

The way in which both Tom and Frank share their faith—as immature or preliminary as it may be—is not uncommon in multiplication. This rapid sharing of the news of Jesus is also a pattern repeated many times over in the Bible. The accounts of the woman at the well in Samaria (John 4), the Gerasene man who Jesus freed from many demons (Mark 5), Zacchaeus the tax collector (Luke 19) and the apostle Paul (Acts 9) are all typical examples.

Many Christians in the West look on this process (especially the rapidity) with skepticism. They question the wisdom of someone so new in the faith—or perhaps not yet even in the faith—being sufficiently qualified. This is natural and expected, given the Western church's emphasis on teaching and education (as described in chapter 1: 'Is It Working?'). If your perspective of spiritual education defaults to a programmatic event with an authorized teacher as the model for spiritual and biblical knowledge, it's natural to presume that it takes years or even decades to be equipped to lead someone else to faith and disciple them.

But the programmatic teaching approach doesn't include a one-on-one discipleship relationship with a personal faith mentor. This relationship includes frequent communication (multiple times per week), training and accountability around things like prayer, reading the Scriptures, and working through questions and application.

I'll speak to this below in more detail, but let me summarize by saying this process works in multiplication because it's based on obedience to the call of God and not on the knowledge level of the person sharing—though knowledge certainly has value. Non-believers both recognize and respond to the evidence and pursuit of genuine faith and belief that are motivated by God's love (and, of course, the working of the Holy Spirit).

> To see the gospel spread so quickly in non-Western cultures speaks more about Western culture than about the validity of frequently and rapidly sharing faith in Christ.

Some of the other key factors that contribute to multiplication are:

- The quality of faith and obedience level of the disciple who is sharing
- The spiritual receptivity and readiness of the person(s) hearing
- The clarity of the call to trust Christ, follow him in obedience, and participate in his kingdom mission
- The pattern and level of mutual accountability established in the discipleship network
- The advance work of the Holy Spirit in the heart of the person hearing—the most important factor of all

Though this frequent and rapid sharing is not typically seen in a Western church cultural context, it's common in other cultures today. We consistently see evidence of it from our networks in multiple locations in Africa, as an example. It's not uncommon for someone who comes to Christ to lead someone else to faith and begin discipling them in twenty-four hours. We have records of this process in multiple networks leading to nine generations of believers in a discipleship chain within twelve months, all with significant evidence of a genuine, maturing faith and obedience to Christ's commands. To see the gospel spread so quickly in non-Western cultures speaks more about Western culture than about the validity of frequently and rapidly sharing faith in Christ.

Multiplication: The Why

Now that we've laid out what multiplication is, let's turn our attention to why it's so important in assessing CAWKI and its effectiveness in accomplishing the mission Christ gave the church.

Relational Investment and Accountability

In a healthy DMM approach, typically one disciple invests significant time in discipling another person(s). This investment involves mutual reading of the Bible, being transparent and accountable with each other for life choices, decisions, dealing with temptation and overcoming sinful habits, obedience to Jesus' commands and way of life, understanding of Scripture and how to study it on their own, as well as resolving issues of theology and doctrinal practices.

At the risk of creating some kind of legalistic yardstick, allow me to offer a sense of context: My personal branch of DMM models and encourages each person to read a significant amount of Scripture (on the order of twenty-five chapters) each week, to do a basic, inductive study of Bible passages each week and to spend significant time in prayer each day (thirty minutes to an hour or more). To many these will sound like legalistic requirements; I assure you they are not. They are life-giving practices that get organically passed from one disciple to another. Each disciple decides how to practice their faith. The consistent and regular practice of these disciplines (along with having a personal faith mentor) equips even people that are new to Christianity relatively quickly and prepares them to disciple others.

This one-to-one (or one-to-few) approach—as opposed to a one-to-many approach—both models and trains the core elements of belief in a way that is accountable and tangible, where each mentor can validate their disciple's readiness to disciple someone else. These qualities simply cannot be achieved in a program-oriented CAWKI approach.

Multiplication vs. Addition

Multiplication is the natural outcome of a one-on-one (or one-on-few) approach to discipleship. This allows for a relatively quick spiritual formation and faith development (when compared to a CAWKI ministry model). It produces subsequent generations of believers that eventually creates a movement of the gospel.

The results come slowly at the beginning, due to the individual approach and the time invested in discipling others until they are equipped to make a disciple. Frankly, the early stages of the process appear low-impact and unimpressive. But over a relatively short amount of time the results speak for themselves.

This can be clearly seen in the illustration of Table 1. Consider on one hand starting with a single follower of Christ who disciples one other person, and over the course of one year equips that person to begin discipling another person. At the end of this year, the first follower is available to disciple another person and the process continues.

This is compared to a megachurch congregation that grows from 0 to 10,000 in weekly worship attendance. This church then plants another campus of 10,000 attenders in the second year, and plants a similar 10,000-attender each year after that.

Keep in mind that discipling one person each year is very reasonable. It takes almost no resources, apart from each person's time, availability, and discipline to continue in the process.

On the other hand, launching a new CAWKI campus of 10,000 each year would be an extremely difficult achievement. As a point of reference, Wikipedia currently lists 109 churches of 10,000 or more in attendance in the U.S., with ten churches of 30,000 or more.[1] This seems impressive at first glance. But bear in mind that it has taken decades for those churches to reach that level of attendance. To grow to 10,000 in a single year has (to my knowledge) never been done in the West. The amount of financial backing, organizational systems and the construction of facilities (even in a multi-campus arrangement) large enough to accommodate the worship and support ministries for a congregation of that size in that short time frame are comically prohibitive.

Year	1 Disciple/Year	10,000 Attenders/Year
1	2	10,000
2	4	20,000
3	8	30,000
4	16	40,000
5	32	50,000
10	1,024	100,000
15	32,768	150,000
20	1,048,576	200,000
25	33,554,432	250,000
30	1,073,741,824	300,000
33	8,589,934,592	330,000

Table 1: Comparing the Results of Multiplication vs. Addition

The point of the illustration is to show how the approach of adding more churches as destinations for people to attend is ineffective—and *massively* so. It will not produce the results necessary to make an impact. Consider that (as of this writing) the population in the U.S. increased by 2,002,609 from the previous year alone (more on this below).[2]

A CAWKI ministry model can never produce multiplication. Section 2: Contrasts, will explain why this is the case. But to summarize the point here, CAWKI—even in its most successful and noteworthy cases, and even when rapidly creating new congregations—is a strategy of addition, not multiplication.

To Overcome Population Growth

As of this writing, global population growth is 1.07–1.08 percent. The U.S., with a current population of over 328 million people, is growing at a slower rate: .62 percent. From 2017–2018 the population in the U.S. grew by slightly over two million people, almost half of which (48 percent) was the result of international migration and the rest through births.[3]

> The approach of adding more churches as destinations for people to attend is ineffective—and massively so. ... CAWKI—even in its most successful and noteworthy cases—is a strategy of addition, not multiplication.

This rate of growth is considerably higher than the growth of churches. To match this growth, there would have to be significantly more churches started. Research from 2000–2004 shows that a net gain of 13,024 churches was required to keep up with the U.S. population growth at the time. But the slow growth rate of churches coupled with the number of churches that closed their doors means we fell short of the mark by 10,000 churches.[4]

Also from that era, researcher Thom Rainer concluded that only 6 percent of the 1,159 U.S. churches his team surveyed in 2002 were growing faster than the communities around them.[5] It should also be noted that this figure does not account for how much of the growth was A) transfer growth from people leaving other congregations, or B) biological growth from people in churches having children.

A more recent study by Rainer confirmed that only 7 percent of Protestant churches place a high value and priority on starting new churches (what he calls "Level 4"), and "the numbers of churches considered multiplying (Level 5: multiple generations of church plants) was 0% in the sample, indicating a negligible number in the total U.S. church population."[6]

The elephant in the room, of course, is that all of the discussion about church growth assumes the churches growing in attendance are also seeing significant numbers of people converting to Christ. But unfortunately that is not the case. A 2018 study performed by LifeWay Research found that not only are 60 percent of Protestant churches plateaued or declining in attendance, more than half saw fewer than ten professions of faith in the past twelve months—and 8 percent had none. Sixty-seven percent of the churches surveyed had fewer than ten per hundred people attending their church. One-third (35 percent) had fewer than five conversions for every hundred people attending their worship services.[7] Fewer and fewer people in the U.S. are adopting and living out the Christian faith—a number that has dropped by eight percentage points from 2007 to 2014 according to Pew Research.[8]

All this data paints a bleak picture of the modern church's effectiveness in reaching the lost and accomplishing the mission Christ gave his followers. If our ministry strategy in the U.S. does not support or produce two-plus million (and growing) new disciples each year, we are falling behind and reducing the influence of the gospel. A DMM approach has the potential to do so because it is built on a strategy of multiplication, where CAWKI is not.

A COVID-19 Observation

The recent pandemic has caught the church in the West completely by surprise, exposing many of the CAWKI assumptions and strategies. In many ways, the legacy church ministry approach was rendered ineffective almost overnight as the opportunity to gather together was taken off the table. In the few short months since COVID hit, there's been a few observable patterns of reaction and response that bear discussion from the context of multiplication.

First, the church largely moved toward trying to replicate it's Sunday experience in a virtual format. The concerns here are many and obvious. The virtual experience, while being readily available, is distant and passive. Chat's in a Facebook Live event or Zoom meeting simply are no substitute for personal interaction. From a leadership standpoint, it has added a layer (or two?) of ambiguity and unknowns to the effort of leading the church members into a vital, disciple-oriented relationship with Christ.

One recent anecdote perfectly captured the tension many pastors are feeling. A legacy church pastor was recalling how analytics show that the average participant in their hour-long virtual Sunday service stayed for only twenty minutes. And to complicate things, there was no way to tell what twenty-minute segment they engaged in. Was it the sermon? The worship? This level of unknowns further complicates an already tenuous situation. How much longer will church members stay engaged when their only involvement is twenty minutes of a virtual service?

Second, many churches suddenly shifted their emphasis toward smaller gatherings (that allow for meeting physical distancing guidelines). There has been a spectrum of responses, from utilizing the existing small group structure to a wholesale shift toward a "house church" emphasis. While this is a natural—and perhaps sensible—response to the immediate crisis of not meeting together in a large group, it doesn't (by itself) promote disciple-making that will create multiplication. It simply miniaturizes the existing tendencies of a CAWKI ministry approach and moves them off campus.

Urgency

The pace of creating disciples matters. Frequency and rapidity of faith sharing and discipleship should be built into the Christian message and experience, because people's eternities are at stake. It should concern us that our neighbors, friends, and family members are not aware of the opportunity to know the truth.

In Western cultures like the U.S., where freedom of religion and religious expression are baked in to our social perspective, the need for urgency can be easily overlooked. Many people consider themselves Christian and attend church because it's a part of their family history or ethnic heritage. Practicing faith often comes down to convenience or preferential choice of a church that best fits a given set of criteria. And in many cases there are multiple church options to choose from. If, for whatever reason, the church we frequent no longer fits the criteria it's a simple (albeit unpleasant) process of choosing another. The process has become so consumerized in the U.S. there's a common term for it: "church-shopping" (which, curiously enough, in my experience is primarily used not by the unchurched but instead by church attenders).

Whether it's due to religion's inclusion into the social fabric or the convenience of multiple church options, the church in the West has lost a sense of urgency. According to Barna Research Group, only 4 percent of unchurched adults were invited to church by a friend and actually went, 23 percent were invited but declined and 73 percent were never invited at all.[9] Meanwhile, the number of adults in the U.S. who claim to be Christian has dropped from 78.4 percent in 2007 to 70.6

percent in 2014. This includes a decline in percentage of Evangelical Protestant population, from 26.3 to 25.4 percent (though they actually increased by two million people). During the same time period, the number of religiously unaffiliated adults has risen six percentage points, from 16.1 to 22.8 percent.[10]

The reasons these data exist are likely complex and multifaceted. My research revealed a wide variety of assumed causes, from spiritual complacency, to the lack of evangelism training, to the lack of responsibility of church leadership ... even to a perspective that Millennials feel it's inappropriate to convince others to change their faith beliefs.[11] Whatever the reasons may be, it's clear that there's a general lack of urgency on the part of the church in the West.

We should take the time to ask some of the big questions this raises.

- Have religious freedom and the vast accessibility of church services desensitized us to the crisis that people all around us are passing into eternity without Christ—all the while being exposed to a smorgasbord of church options to choose from?
- As ambassadors for Christ, have our message and methods of offering the good news of salvation become stale, overused, or ineffective, to the point that our society resents them? And if so, how do we respond?
- Do we assume our methods are right, and our society is the problem?
- Have we given up, lost interest, or been distracted from our mission?
- Is the way we live our faith standing out to those who might be looking for God?
- Is the quality of our love notable? Visible?

How much longer do we continue with our current paradigm and practice of church before we are motivated to change?

Multiplication and Strategy

Multiplication is a natural result of a persistent, prioritized strategy to make disciples that can make disciples. When we apply the biblical principles consistently and intentionally, people will share and invest time with others and encourage them to pass on the knowledge, commitment, and calling of being a disciple and making more disciples.

The implication of this is both simple and profound: We don't have to figure out how to make multiplication happen. We do, however, have to identify and remove the barriers that prevent multiplication from naturally occurring. The hard pill to swallow is that the way we currently practice church in the West creates—however unintentionally—a number of these barriers.

Have religious freedom and the vast accessibility of church services desensitized us to the crisis that people all around us are passing into eternity without Christ—all the while being exposed to a smorgasbord of church options to choose from?

In effect, CAWKI is getting in the way of making disciples.

I realize this statement can appear threatening and inflammatory. I know this because of the challenges we encounter when explaining the merits of DMM and multiplication to people who are deeply invested in CAWKI. Typically, the arguments against them fall into one or more of these broad assumptions:

- **Error and heresy**—A DMM approach opens the door for error and encourages heresy. Because of relatively young believers in the faith mentoring and discipling a lost person, it can easily turn into "the blind leading the blind."
- **Lack of control**—The lack of a trained, authorized pastor in the individual churches in a network means there's little to no control over what happens.

- **Lack of congregational teaching**—The DMM approach does not include a weekly, congregation-wide gathering for teaching/preaching.
- **A small group can't be a church**—Usually these concerns focus around the lack of organizational components deemed necessary in order to be a biblically-authorized church (elders/deacons, a senior pastor, a weekly gathering of the entire body, etc.).

The reactions above are intended to point out DMM's weaknesses, but unknowingly they are actually attempts to defend CAWKI methodologies. They are activations of the bias for the current church paradigm which assumes CAWKI is the best and only church model. In essence, these arguments say, "DMM is not how church is done, so it can't be right."

The concerns above are certainly viable. But the irony is that the CAWKI ministry model doesn't even prevent them. If it did, all of the churches in the West would be doctrinally sound, biblically-based, spiritually healthy, and functional—and we know this is not the case.

Let me assure you: I recognize and share in the concerns raised above. My point is there are ways to achieve the intent and purpose of

> **Church as it's currently practiced in the West is not the only model for church, and—if multiplication is the desired outcome—it is in fact an inferior model.**

the CAWKI structures and processes by using different methods—we simply need to allow ourselves the opportunity to explore them.

Multiplication is happening right now around the world, and has been happening in increasing rates for the last twenty-plus years. The 24:14 Coalition tracks disciple-multiplying movements around the world. A "movement" is an intentional, organized network of disciple-making relationships that has reached multiple generations.

Of particular importance are movements that have reached five generations, an indication of healthy disciple-making.

The largest percentage of these documented movements are in South Asia and now more recently in sub-Saharan Africa, the most mature of which began two to three decades ago and now include hundreds of millions of believers. The areas lagging behind in numbers of disciple-multiplying movements are the culturally Western continents of the Pacific (Australia, New Zealand, Melanesia, Micronesia) and the Americas. These movements have now spread to cover every continent and include 74.1 million believers. What's most interesting about 24:14's data, however, is the number of these movements have been increasing—rapidly: Over the last two years, the number of movements with five-plus generations has increased from around 200 to now over 1,000.[12]

A premise of this book is that church as it's currently practiced in the West is not the only model for church, and—if multiplication is the desired outcome—it is in fact an inferior model. The next section of the book, 'Part 2: Contrasts', will work through twenty-five aspects of ministry to show the differences between DMM and CAWKI and explain how the latter actually prevents discipleship multiplication from occurring.

Also, as a reminder, I am not suggesting we abandon CAWKI methods altogether or immediately. That would be too radical of an organizational change to navigate in a healthy way. There are some elements of CAWKI that are positive and helpful. But before we can fully understand how to manage changing a CAWKI ministry wisely and strategically, we have to be willing to first take a sober assessment of this model to realize both its shortcomings and its strengths.

Part 2:
Contrasts

Five areas of the legacy church model
with twenty-five separate ministry approaches
that effectively block multiplication from occurring,
contrasted with the disciple-multiplying movement
approach that encourages and establishes
multiplication

5 Who the Church Is

Spiritual identity means we are not what we do or what people say about us. And we are not what we have. We are the beloved daughters and sons of God.

—Henri Nouwen

The concept of identity is foundational. If you don't know who you are or aspire to be, how can you ever be effective or fulfilled in what you do? How can you truly know if you are making progress or be assured the direction in which you're progressing is the right one?

The contrasts between CAWKI and DMM—both at the organizational and the individual participant levels—become immediately evident when viewed through the lens of identity.

Church Identity Contrasts

1 — Organizational Identity:
   Location vs. People

2 — Orientation to the World:
   Come vs. Go

3 — Organizing Principle:
   Differentiation vs. Unity

4 — Organizational Structure:
   Hierarchy vs. Network

5 — People's Self-Perception:
   Adherent vs. Disciple-Maker

Contrast #1 – Organizational Identity: Location vs. People

If you search for "church" on Dictionary.com, the first definition you will see is "a building for public Christian worship." In my experience, this speaks to what is far and away the most common perception people in the West have about church— whether they are Christians or not. They identify church by a location, and to a lesser extent a senior minister (especially true for large or prominent congregations) and/or a denominational affiliation. This seemingly innocuous and nuanced identity actually has enormous ramifications on accomplishing the mission Christ gave us.

The Church as a Location

There are several significant implications with identifying the church as a location. The first will be addressed more fully in *Contrast #2 – Orientation to the World: Come vs. Go.* The building cannot go anywhere. Buildings, high-profile individuals or even denominations do not reproduce themselves readily or quickly, which contributes in a significant way to entrenching a "come" orientation into your methodology and practice.

The second implication is more subtle, but ultimately more damaging to the mission of making disciples. If individual believers view the church as the collective of all that happens in the building and in the associated programming, then they view themselves as spectators at an event or participants in a program. The event or the program itself ultimately becomes the driving method of faith practice. If they see themselves as adherents to a visible and influential pastor, then the pastor becomes the voice of authority.

It all creates a subtle dependency in which the individual believer pulls back from full engagement in the Great Commission. They become inoculated against the call to go and make disciples: They get just enough of a shot of faith and the experience of being with the community of believers that they don't have to step out any further in faith or hear the voice of God during the rest of the week when they aren't "at church."

When all the processes and systems reward and incentivize identifying church as the location, it's only natural that believers' lives ultimately become segmented with a line drawn between the sacred and the secular. This segmentation makes it more of a challenge for followers of Christ to act as the church out among those who need the gospel most—outside the building and its associated programming.

> Individual believers ... become inoculated against the call to go and make disciples: They get just enough of a shot of faith and the experience of being with the community of believers that they don't have to step out any further in faith or hear the voice of God.

The Church as the People

By contrast, in a disciple-multiplying movement the church is identified as the people who claim faith in Jesus, the collection of the followers of Christ around the world—wherever they happen to go—and not the *place* they congregate. The implication being: Wherever the people go, that's where the church is and the gates of hell will not prevail against them. It supports an understanding that believers take the full authority of Christ and the presence of the Holy Spirit living inside them wherever they go.

Followers of Christ are his ambassadors (1 Cor. 5:20) that carry the "ministry of reconciliation" with them. God is using us as the delivery vehicle for his personal message and appeal for the world to be reconciled to him. As ambassadors, we have the delegated authority to speak on God's behalf and to conduct the ministry of reconciliation as his representatives. It is an immense and invaluable ministry, and having that level of responsibility and authorization stewarded to us is sobering. Without a doubt we should use it responsibly and by faith, but we *should* use it—and putting believers in a disciple-making network gives them more opportunity to. In fact, its success hinges upon it.

Believers have the authority to preach, teach, evangelize, heal, pray, to bring the full authority and weight of the Kingdom of God against the powers and principalities of darkness seeking to keep the world in a state of spiritual fog and blindness. This simple perspective on faith engages people to be bold in their evangelism and trust in the leading of the Holy Spirit.

This truth is unfortunately de-emphasized or even dispelled in many Protestant circles in the West. This has come to be a point of personal repentance for me. Years ago I would have discouraged believers from focusing on the more miraculous signs of the Holy Spirit that can accompany expansion of the kingdom, such as healings. I did this, to a large extent, because of what I perceive to be abuses and an unbalanced, hyper-focus on the miraculous signs by some elements of the church. But if I'm honest, I would also say I didn't have the simple, child-like faith necessary to believe God would call me to pray for someone to be healed as a sign to demonstrate to them God's power and ability to reconcile them to himself.

I'm not advocating that we elevate signs and wonders as the target of faith. But I am suggesting that in the West we have diminished or discouraged believers from acting in simple faith, believing and expecting God will do miracles to break the bonds of sin and blindness to the gospel. He did it in the Scriptures; and he's doing it regularly in so many other places around the world today.

Instead of viewing church as the place and the program where faith practices occur, believers in a DMM view themselves as the church—the faithful people, individually and collectively, that God works in and through to accomplish his reconciling work. They don't have to defer to the limitations of a prescribed program. Every believer's life is appropriately on mission, where each of us is a missionary to the lost world around us.

Contrast #2 – Orientation to the World:
Come vs. Go

"Where do you go to church?"

It's the common way people in the West ask about church affiliation. The phrase itself demonstrates the common perception, by both Christians and the society at large, that church as we know it in the West means congregations in fixed locations. Their buildings are static, not portable. Their activities happen on established days, in programmed fashion, at predetermined and scheduled time slots. It is a destination people must come to if they are seeking God or interested in spiritual matters and want to intersect with him.

Come

This "come" mentality is more than just a physical or programmatic identity, however. It is born out of a perception that the church is an institution, woven into the fabric of society in a given city or town. Like the grocery store, the post office, city hall, the YMCA, the movie theater, the doctor's office or hospital … you'd expect to find institutions and organizations like these in any municipality in the West. And the bigger the city, the more diversity you'd expect to find.

Part of the CAWKI paradigm also includes being viewed as a social service provider, offering spiritual services for those inclined to participate or those who have affinity with it. Occasionally, it provides broader services like performing marriages or burial needs, hospital visitation, etc., for people who aren't officially affiliated with a specific congregation.

This identity has been around for as long as the United States has been in existence. It's a natural progression of the paradigm we inherited from Western Europe, which itself was received from the established practices of the Roman Catholic church before it (as discussed in chapter 3: "How We Got Here"). Because it's our heritage, we've never really asked ourselves a vital question: How does this "come" identity align with Jesus' command to "go" into all the world and make disciples?

A "come" orientation to the world can easily create a barrier mindset, a subtle pride and judgmental attitude that distances believers from those who most need the gospel. It is the same mindset that settled into the Jewish national identity seen in the Old Testament. It can reinforce an internally-focused attitude, where the primary concern is on ourselves and our congregation. This attitude separates us from those who need the gospel the most—perhaps unintentionally, but the separation is real enough to create a barrier.

How does this "come" identity align with Jesus' command to "go" into all the world and make disciples?

Go

In contrast, a "go" orientation actively puts believers out among the harvest of lost people, as missionaries to their culture and network of relationships. Those far from Christ hear the story of God and his redemption in their own setting, not the setting of a church that may be foreign to them. These people are then able to take the message to a third group of people in their own words, without having to couch it in the context of church. They don't have to first "fit in" to the language, culture, and programmed expression of the church.

Perhaps most significantly, a "go" orientation to the world is an object lesson to those who come to Christ, emphasizing that believers are all called to be disciple-makers. With this orientation, going becomes the normal, expected practice modeled and supported as new generations of believers come to know the Lord and practice their faith.

Contrast #3 – Organizing Principle: Differentiation vs. Unity

It is common practice in the Western church to distinguish our congregations from each other because of difference in practices and/or beliefs. Western Christians seeking information on an unfamiliar church know to navigate to the *What We Believe* page to determine its stance on their prioritized theological or doctrinal positions. Denominations tell the story of their tradition's founders and where or how it all began. New churches, trying to separate themselves stylistically from existing churches, talk about how they are different.

Have you ever stopped to wonder why this is so accepted and what impact this might be having on our communication of the gospel? What does it say to a lost world that we highlight that which separates us instead of that which brings us together? How can we, with integrity, call people to turn the other cheek and love their enemy when we won't fellowship with other believers in Christ—whom we will worship with in eternity before the throne of God?

What is the impact on disciples made in this environment?

What Keeps Us Apart
Division in the Western Protestant church has been a regular theme throughout its history. The emphasis on denominationalism, the hardening of theological viewpoints and the common practice of churches

splitting over unreconciled differences has positioned us against each other. The practical gulf separating Anglo and African-American congregations remains active even though most of the racial issues causing the divide seems to have been removed.

When the church's organizing principle is highlighting a faith distinctive, doctrinal position, denominational heritage, polity, ethnic heritage, etc., it positions us against each other and prolongs the subtle state of division in the West. Entire segments of the church choose not to fellowship with each other over such issues, and many times end up in emotionally charged debates where we criticize and judge each other publicly.

Division is a luxury often associated with freedom from persecution. Consider what would happen to the church in the West if overnight it were to lose its privileged status; if faith in Christ were to become illegal with penalties of ostracism, loss of employment, privilege or social standing, or even imprisonment or death. Most Westerners can't even conceive of such a scenario (though this is a daily reality for many believers in other parts of the world today). In such conditions, differentiation like we see in CAWKI today would be so petty as to be laughable.

To be fair, we inherited the form of church we know and practice; what we know as normal is all we've ever known. From that perspective, I give Western Christianity some grace. That said, the time has come for us to soberly and objectively consider the nature and extent of the divided state we continue to embrace.

Think of it this way: When was the last time you heard of a CAWKI congregation promoting their unity with all the churches that follow Christ? I must admit, at one point my pride would have viewed such a statement of unity with skepticism, likely branding such a church as some kind of ecumenical group that believes in everything (which ultimately means they believe in nothing). Yet such a statement of unity was exactly Jesus' prayer for us in John 17: to be unified as He and the Father are unified.

We would do well to accept that we divide the church in the West because we can and because we choose to; it is simply more convenient than resolving our differences and choosing to "be perfected in unity" (John 17:23). Jesus prayed for us, hoping we might all be one—as He and the Father are one—so the world may know that he (Jesus) was the Father-sent Savior of the world and the true depth of God's love would be revealed.

What Keeps Us Together

When the church's organizing principle is unity of our common faith in Jesus Christ and accomplishing the Great Commission, our actions all stem from a single, primary purpose. All the small differences—in belief, practice, tradition, style, interpretation, ethnicity, culture, generational perspectives, etc.—become secondary and unimportant.

In my own life, intentionally practicing this unity has been a truly unique experience.[1] I've found that the doctrinal or theological questions I consistently dealt with in legacy church settings rarely materialize in our particular DMM network. Topics that were frequently controversial in legacy settings—

> We would do well to accept that we divide the church in the West because we can and because we choose to; it is simply more convenient than resolving our differences and choosing to "be perfected in unity" (John 17:23).

like election, assurance of salvation, end times interpretations, and the validity of the "sign" gifts—rarely occur when the primary focus is disciple-making.

When they do, they are usually well downstream in the disciple-making process. We then address them in a balanced and fair way, explaining the different perspectives and traditions as options to consider as best we can. We place them appropriately below the priorities of making disciples and fulfilling the "law of love" laid out in Romans chapters 13 and 14: Loving each other in a non-judgmental manner. We strive to recognize we are in a loving partnership with fellow members in the diverse body of Christ that view and practice some parts of their faith differently, without imposing our views upon each other.

When our emphasis is on loving God, loving others, and making disciples, the issues simply aren't as important—and they are only divisive when we allow them to be. The disciple-making mission gives our differences their appropriate context. It's refreshing to be in a room of people with very different theological perspectives, praying, worshipping, planning, sharing resources, and encouraging one another in accomplishing the task our Lord appointed to us. This approach isn't as theologically clean and tidy; or as easy, for that matter. But it feels a lot like the New Testament. And frankly, most of the issues that seem so primary to CAWKI church distinctives aren't that important to those who are desperate to meet Jesus.

Disagreements among the saints who live and minister in a fallen world are a reality, especially considering that we hold strongly to our deeply personal beliefs and faith convictions. Clearly, disagreements don't necessarily qualify as division, and there are precedents in Scripture for disagreement and breaking off of joint ministry effort.[2] There isn't a firm demarcation between disagreement and division, and in fact it may likely be a matter of semantics.

So let us be clear: The goal with unity is not a lack of disagreement, but to handle our disagreement in a way that "maintains the unity of the Spirit in the bond of peace" (Eph. 4:3). Can we disagree in such a way that our mutual love and concern for one another aren't compromised?

Unity is something all believers are called to live out at every level of organization, whether it's marriage or family, groups of believers, a local congregation or the universal collection of believers from all nations and cultures. Unity is only possible through complete humility and gentleness with each other (Eph. 4:2). We cannot attain unity while also maintaining prideful, critical, and judgmental attitudes. To experience unity we must stop promoting the things that contribute to division. We must find a way to discuss the important matters of faith in a way that promotes unity above our own interests.

Think of it this way: The next time you recite the Lord's Prayer, keep your own practice of unity in mind when you say, "Your kingdom come, on earth as it is in heaven." If we expect to be unified in heaven, worshipping together as one before the throne of God for all eternity, shouldn't we be unified here—now—so God can in fact answer our prayer?

As we approach the hoped-for return of our Savior, how powerful would it be if the church who calls upon his name—with its many perspectives and practices—unified itself around a common cause and purpose? What would it say to a lost world searching for the truth of God?

Contrast #4 – Organizational Structure: Hierarchy vs. Network

When it comes to the organizational structure of the church, there is an overarching strategic question we must ask ourselves: What's the most effective way to organize people toward the desired outcome of making disciples of all nations?

97

The legacy church in the West is typically organized in hierarchical form, with a senior minister at the top of the org chart (often aided by a board of directors) and a team of staff and volunteers underneath. This structure is borrowed other from Western organizations, primarily civil government, military, and (more recently) commercial companies. It became more widely established in the time following Constantine when the church became the state religion of the Roman Empire and the authority of the bishops entrenched at the city and regional levels. As the exclusivity of the priesthood was established and priests were the only ones capable of performing the Christian sacraments, it became normal for each church—now mapped out in geographical dioceses across cities—to fall under the administration of a priest with deacons underneath him.

In contrast, the early church (in the first two centuries) operated as a network. It was decentralized, and operated with a broad leadership base that relied on collaborative unity and input from those with recognized, demonstrated leadership gifts, authority, and experience.

A Hierarchical Structure

A hierarchical organizational structure does have some advantages: It allows for clearer lines of reporting, oversight, and order. When managed well, it works fine for specific functions, like military operations or bringing a product to market.

But it has some disadvantages, particularly when it comes to the desired outcome of multiplication. A hierarchical structure is static, inflexible, and complex; it has multiple layers of management, authority, decision-making, and bureaucracy. In fact, it's not uncommon for companies who've realized this to attempt to "flatten" their organization by reducing multiple layers of middle management that slow down operations and production.

Another disadvantage is that authority becomes centralized in a single person, who then dispenses it as needed down the management tree (see *Contrast #12* on page 128 for more on this). This is such an issue that some of the most popular leadership books being published today deal with employee engagement: how to motivate and empower the workforce so the lowest ranks in the organization are tangibly fulfilled. It is a challenge in many companies to create an environment where employees feel they are making a genuine, significant contribution to the overall effort.

A hierarchical organization is also inefficient. Approval from a higher authority is required before new actions can be taken. Decisions must be communicated up the chain for vetting and input. In the process, decision-making authority resides in fewer and fewer people, and typically further away from the operation. As the hierarchical organization grows the senior leader spends more time with organizational management issues. Continued growth creates the odd irony that the senior leader leads and speaks for the organization but has a decreasing practical knowledge of what's happening in the lower levels.

Network Structure

A network organization is more agile and adaptable. Individual believers are equipped to carry out the mission of the church wherever and whenever the opportunity presents itself. Because each "node" in the network is able to execute the mission in its context, it does not need the input of another decision-making authority before taking action. When it encounters a situation where additional input is appropriate or necessary, it can take advantage of the broad accessibility of the network and bring in the closest and most appropriate resource to deal with the issue at hand. Leadership is present in the network and is available to communicate and support nodes along the network as needed.

It's also much easier and fluid for people in a network—and leaders across network organizations—to collaborate. Personally speaking, in my coaching experience I find that collaboration is not a Western cultural strength. Particularly in the U.S., with our well-entrenched individualistic worldview, we find it more difficult to share ideas, to defer to others, to be vulnerable or transparent, to receive input or critique from others, to admit failure or do anything that might weaken our social position. And yet all of these things are essential for collaboration to occur.[3] In a network organization, where the mission is the unifying goal, there are no relative levels or hierarchy to "slot" ourselves above or below others. There is less competitive and individualistic inertia to overcome.

The U.S. military's experience in fighting against Al Qaeda and Taliban forces demonstrates the effectiveness of a network organization. As Ori Brafman and Rod Beckstrom demonstrate in their book *The Starfish and the Spider*, The U.S. and its allies found the Al Qaeda network to be a worthy foe, despite its vast inferiority in technology, training, and equipment. Killing or capturing a senior leader in the network did little to disrupt operational effectiveness. Each terrorist cell knew the overall vision and mission, and within certain broad guidelines were free to operate as they saw fit to accomplish it.[4] I don't want to imply that a hierarchical leadership structure in and of itself is worldly and prone to evil; if it were Jesus would have commanded us not to use it.[5] There are many organizations and companies utilizing an executive leadership and management structure that are skillfully and wonderfully led, values-driven with amazingly positive cultures.

I do, however, want to emphasize that hierarchical structure is a Western organizational trait. It is a common cultural perception and experience seen in the marketplace, in politics, in the military ... it is virtually everywhere—and it's what we are accustomed to; it's our default. But changing the church's structure is possible, if there is commitment toward unity and operating effectively in a network structure. Just because we don't typically use it doesn't mean we can't—or shouldn't—use it.

A hierarchical structure has both advantages and disadvantages. It's not that there's a right and a wrong way to structure an organization. There are only outcomes and consequences, limitations and advantages. Organizational structure, in and of itself, is not a spiritual issue; it is a people organization issue. If the desired outcome is multiplication, then a hierarchical structure will be a limiting factor; a network structure will not.

Contrast #5 – People's Self-Perception: Adherent vs. Disciple-Maker

How people see themselves is their identity: who they think they are or who they think they should be; their personal sense of self. Identity is formed over time through a variety of inputs, such as values, experiences, roles played, relationships, etc. Identity plays a powerful—and often hidden—role in human behavior.

If we view our identity positively (i.e., we accept and agree it is who we aspire to be) our behavior will likely align with and support our identity. The harmony between identity and behavior produces a level of comfort and satisfaction.

Human behavioral psychology is much more complex and nuanced than this, of course. But for the sake of this discussion it is helpful to simplify it because the way the church functions plays a part in shaping believers' identity.

This topic is somewhat more obscure and complex than practical and measurable, but it's no less real. And it's important because self-perception will either contribute to or detract from disciple-making.

Being Church-Going Christians

CAWKI reinforces an adherent identity in the congregation, where people see themselves conforming to the church organization as the primary agency in their spiritual health, growth, and practice. Participants identify themselves as supporters of the organization, at whatever levels they may identify with the most: the denomination, the senior pastor, the worship style, ministry emphasis, or even the way of life or established behaviors.

The structures and processes of church convey to participants that they are expected to support the church, the pastoral staff, and its ministry philosophy. They are to abide by the church's ordinances, methods, and policies and remain members in good standing. If and when they cannot or will not adhere, the most generally accepted course of action is to leave the church to find another they can adhere to.

That may sound extreme or cultic at face value, which of course is not what I'm suggesting. But I am highlighting that the operation and organization of church is such that Christians in the West view themselves as adherents to it.

Protestantism upholds the concept of the priesthood of all believers: Individual followers of Jesus have the competency and privilege to interact with God directly without the need for a mediator. But the way CAWKI is organized and functions doesn't fully support this identity. However slight or accidental it may be, it retains a vestige of the old Catholic Church's sacerdotal heritage where the priests were seen as divine mediators between God and the people.

When the systems, programs, and overall experience of church encourages and reinforces this adherent identity, there is little opportunity or support for people to see themselves as disciple-makers. Without the clarity around this personal identity there's little motivation for them to be a disciple that takes responsibility for training and equipping someone else to be a disciple.

Being Disciple-Makers

A DMM approach reinforces the identity—the calling—of being an active disciple-maker. It removes the organization of church and its mediatorial role, and instead encourages followers of Jesus to hear directly from God, following the commands of Christ and the empowering of the Holy Spirit. The organization can, of course, provide much-needed resources, training, support, encouragement, etc. But the primary identity of those professing faith in Christ is that of a viable, Spirit-led, disciple-making disciple; not merely an adherent. This identity motivates believers to accept the challenge and responsibility to lead someone else

> Those who follow him will see themselves differently, and this new identity creates a dissatisfaction with our current behavior until it is changed to align with the new identity.

to faith in Christ and walk with them as they grow in their faith development.

You quickly learn as a disciple-maker that DMM is a spiritually empowered, divinely ordained process. It is not a program or a methodology to be adopted. While there are patterns and methods involved, each conversation with people is different. God shows up in unique ways as you go about announcing his kingdom and looking for those who are responding to God. If we attempt to make disciples

103

by adhering to what amounts to a Christian recipe, it simply won't reproduce the fruit of generational discipleship. It becomes merely another mechanism to adhere to.

It's also interesting that Jesus gave specific effort to forming and reforming his disciples' identities. He said he would make them "fishers of people" (Matt. 4:19); he changed the nature of his relationship with them from "servants to friends" (John 15:15). In the Sermon on the Mount he cast vision around the identities of those who would be in the kingdom of God: the meek, the peacemakers, the pure-in-heart, the righteousness-hungry, etc. As the rest of the Sermon indicates, it's not just people who acted meekly, peacefully, pure, etc. Those who follow him will see themselves differently. This new identity creates a dissatisfaction with our current behavior until it is changed to align with the new identity. Only those who see themselves this way can love their enemy, be non-judgmental, and live not for themselves but instead live wisely on the commands of Jesus.

CAWKI can call believers to adopt this new identity, too. But it cannot support the application of this identity the way a DMM approach can.

6   What the Church Does

There is nothing worse than a sharp image of a fuzzy concept.

—Ansel Adams

The church's activity is an outflow of its identity (see the previous chapter). Our activity is a reflection of our values and the things we believe to be important and true.

Here we look at how the church goes about setting ministry goals and practicing its philosophy of ministry.

> **Church Action Contrasts**
>
> 6 – Ministry Goal:
>
>   Salvations vs. Disciple-Makers
>
> 7 – Primary Method:
>
>   Teaching vs. Training
>
> 8 – Growth Strategy:
>
>   Fast vs. Slow
>
> 9 – Key Metric:
>
>   Attenders vs. Capable Disciple-Makers
>
> 10 – Ministry Application:
>
>   Programmatic vs. Personal
>
> 11 – Primary Meeting Structure:
>
>   Congregation vs. Small Group

Contrast #6 – Ministry Goal:
Salvations vs. Disciple-Makers

One of the hallmarks of the evangelical Protestant church has been its emphasis on individual, personal salvation in Christ. It has served as the primary motivating goal for both individual believers and churches alike. It is viewed as the standard indicator of allegiance to and faith in Christ, especially since the time of the Great Awakenings. Conversions and baptisms are easily the most celebrated metrics of the ministry efforts for the Western church.

Without a doubt, salvation in Christ is an appropriately important milestone and we should see each individual's decision to follow Jesus in faith as a point of celebration. But viewing salvations as the targeted outcome of the church's ministry also blurs some very important realities that should be kept clear.

Emphasizing Conversion

The most significant reality is the practical mission of the church in the West (to help people get saved) is not Christ's stated mission for the church (to go and make disciples). They are obviously related—after all, Jesus included baptizing disciples as a part the Great Commission. But they are very different goals, and accomplishing those goals requires very different activities, competencies, processes, and measurements.

Not only are they different goals, they are actually different concepts altogether. Making disciples is a developmental process, where salvations are an outcome. But this distinction is lost when we emphasize personal professions of faith without also providing the surrounding context of being a disciple-maker.

In elevating salvations we inadvertently reduce their significance as they come to be seen as a uniquely isolated and individual event. Salvation should be seen as critical step in the development of a person who is on the way to becoming a faithful, mature, capable, disciple-making follower of Christ who is a member of the global and universal community of believers.

The final reality is we should be concerned that many (if not most) Christians in the West might assume that being saved means they're a disciple. Consider the implications of the legacy church's centuries-old message of the gospel that might go something like: "Repent of your sins, and trust in Jesus as your personal Lord and Savior in order to receive eternal life." Being a disciple—much less being a disciple-maker—simply isn't present in this message; at best it's implied or tangentially included.

> The practical mission of the church in the West (to help people get saved) is not Christ's stated mission for the church (to go and make disciples).

We must be honest with ourselves and admit that a balanced reading of the gospels does not allow for the conclusion that Jesus promoted merely a commitment to an intellectual choice for eternal security in heaven as an alternative to eternal condemnation and separation from God. Instead, Jesus defined a disciple as one who surrenders their life (present and future) and reorients themselves to His teachings and habits, *and then teaches these to others in a way that allows them to do the same.*

Emphasizing Discipleship
In the documentary *Sheep Among Wolves,* highlighting the growing DMM of the church in the Middle East, one church leader made a clear and profound statement that speaks directly to this issue: "The church in the West converts [in order] to disciple, but in DMM we disciple [in order] to convert." Meaning, in a DMM approach the effort focuses on discipleship as the process of following Jesus and living as he lived—a process that includes trusting Christ for personal salvation.

Think of it this way: If the targeted outcome of your church's ministry is equipping people to be disciple-makers, then salvations will be appropriately included in the results as a key milestone in their development. But if your target is salvations, you may or may not see your people become disciple-makers (unless you emphasize this through another ministry focus).

This topic overlaps with a number of other contrasts highlighted in 'Part 2: Contrasts', namely:

- The way Christians see themselves and their life purpose (see *Contrast #5* on page 101)
- The priority of training (see *Contrast #7* on page 108)
- The corporate practice of measuring disciple-makers (see *Contrast #9* on page 115)
- The invitation to a call (see *Contrast #16* on page 152)
- The importance of obedience in the practice of faith (see *Contrast #19* on page 161 andsee *Contrast #21* on page 172)
- The engagement of people in the discipleship process immediately—even prior to conversion to Christ (see *Contrast #23* on page 181)

This concept of salvation in Christ is best understood if it is examined in the entire context of discipleship and not as a stand-alone event. This holistic emphasis should help individual followers of Christ understand the opportunity, necessity, and urgency to both be a disciple and to disciple others.

Contrast #7 – Primary Method:
Teaching vs. Training

A method describes the manner in which we go about our activities; it's an order or system. Analyzing a method will reveal underlying assumptions, motivations, expectations, and beliefs that sometimes we're aware of but in many cases we never question. Analyzing methods can also reveal actions and behaviors we weren't aware we were doing because we simply never evaluated our methodology—we just kept doing what had always been done.

When looking at the most common corporate practices of the legacy church in the West, it becomes apparent that teaching is the primary method being deployed. This has some significant implications on how disciples of Jesus are made.

Teaching as THE Essential Activity

Consider how widely and often teaching is expressed in the average Protestant CAWKI congregation. To begin with, the sermon is easily the most prominent aspect of the weekly gathering. The entire service is built around it and it usually consumes the largest block of time. Children's programming typically utilizes educational, age-appropriate, curriculum-based methods and processes. We encourage believers to participate in supplemental Bible study, whether it's in Sunday School, in church-sponsored groups during the week, on their own, or in outside ministries like Bible Study Fellowship. Many Christians have additional learning intake from popular Bible teaching videos or podcasts.

> CAWKI pastors teach so frequently and at such an advanced level that they've set an example very few people in the congregation can follow.

Considering what's not included in the legacy church's activities also provides some insight. My experience is that many churches don't emphasize discipleship. They don't have discipleship programs or processes in place, they don't promote discipleship or the qualities of a disciple of Christ. Churches that do emphasize discipleship often do so in an educational context, like attending a class or participating in a study. "Discipling" in a legacy context often means assisting someone who's already a Christian reach higher levels of understanding in their biblical, doctrinal, or theological knowledge.

CAWKI can inspire, exhort, encourage, and inform—primarily through large group events or through other media—to highlight the importance of things like personal knowledge of Jesus, experiencing God, and maintaining a relationship with him. But it is limited in how it can practically support people in living out Jesus' commands and teachings in daily life. There are precious few mechanisms in place to provide effective modeling, coaching, mentoring, and accountability.

As a whole, the legacy Protestant church teaches quite well. CAWKI pastors teach so frequently and at such an advanced level that they've set an example very few people in the congregation can follow. Consider what message it sends to congregants when teaching is so highly prioritized corporately but discipleship is not. It shouldn't surprise us that so few legacy church congregants consistently and actively engage in disciple-making.

It would seem that CAWKI's emphasis on teaching is grounded in the assumption that knowledge is the key to faithfully following Jesus' teachings and example.[1] Of course, biblical and doctrinal education are important. But is education the essential ingredient for equipping people to follow Jesus? How much teaching is necessary to equip someone to make another disciple?

Teaching as AN Essential Activity

The primary method for a disciple-multiplying movement is based on training—which involves teaching, but it also involves many more elements. The goal is not just to educate, but to equip people to be disciple-makers as consistently and quickly as possible. This is something almost anyone can do and all Christians are called to do, whatever their level of skill or giftedness.

It's developmental, not unlike many other processes that involve repetitive practice to gain competency. Think of the way we learn other things in life that are more than just intellectual knowledge: Golf, woodworking, martial arts, painting, riding a bike, gardening, public speaking, scuba diving, etc. You would never expect people to be proficient in these activities by listening to a speaker talk about them. Instead, you would teach a concept, then demonstrate, then let them try it. After some correction and focused advice, you let them try it again until they reach a base level of competency. Then you move on to the next concept and repeat the process. The same is true for training someone to disciple others.

Teaching is only one aspect of discipleship, and as surprising as this may sound it's not the most important. I encourage you to read the gospels and compare the number of times Jesus emphasized obeying his commands versus learning the Scriptures. Review Jesus' comments to the professional experts of the Old Testament, the teachers, scribes, and Pharisees, and see how Jesus chastised them for their lack of obedience of the Scriptures they claimed to know so well.

> **Think of the way we learn other things in life that are more than just intellectual knowledge: Golf, woodworking, martial arts, painting, riding a bike, gardening, public speaking, scuba diving, etc. You would never expect people to be proficient in these activities by listening to a speaker talk about them.**

In presenting this contrast I feel compelled to assure you of my own personal belief in the validity and value of teaching the Word of God. First of all, teaching is my primary personal gift of the five APEST gifts (described in see *Contrast #14* on page 139). Anyone who knows me well will affirm this.

Most importantly, however, is my own faith story and how God used the Bible to save me. I met Jesus through the pages of the Scriptures as I read them for the first time alone in my apartment as a young adult. I stumbled across Galatians 2:21 and gave my life to God on the spot. I realized my life-long ambition of doing the right thing had zero value in making me righteous, and was in fact the reason I was shackled with the guilt I was experiencing.

Please believe me when I say that I hold the Bible—from knowing it, to studying it and teaching others how to do the same—in the highest regard. I am convicted that teaching is good and necessary, but I am even more convicted that teaching at the expense of training people to make disciples blocks multiplication.

For further impact on this topic, please see *Contrast #13 – Maturity Gauge: Knowledge vs. Christlikeness* (page 136) and *Contrast #22 – Interaction: Knowledge Sharing vs. Mutual Accountability* (page 177).

Contrast #8 – Growth Strategy: Fast vs. Slow

Our Western culture values production and rapid growth. A popular phrase often used in the marketplace summarizes the entire mindset: "Getting stuff done" (except with a different "s" word). We multi-task, trying to fit more productivity into our available time—which seems to be eroding at a much faster rate than it used to.

With this as our cultural backdrop, it has become normal to both presume and expect that bigger and faster is better. This fast-paced, growth-oriented, get-stuff-done, productivity mindset dramatically impacts the way we view the disciple-making process.

Go Fast

One of the primary concerns of a CAWKI ministry approach is a focus on attendance, as presented in chapter 1. The productivity mindset fuels a drive to increase attendance, along with the seemingly common-sense reasoning that increasing attendance at a fast rate is better than a slower rate. A church that's growing quickly is interpreted as more people potentially coming to faith and an affirmation of everything from programming effectiveness to God's blessing. It creates a more energetic environment for worship and it allows the church to do more.

We celebrate and elevate churches that grow quickly, giving them special status and presenting them as models for other churches to follow. This is understandable, given the amount of effort required to grow a church—particularly a new one. As a former pastor in a CAWKI ministry setting I can attest to the drive to grow my ministry, and the faster the better.

Go Slow to Go Fast

In contrast with this is the DMM approach where the goal in making a disciple is not speed, it's quality—specifically: sufficient quality to be able to pass on *all* the healthy traits of being a disciple. If we don't maintain this level of quality, nothing else we do will make any difference because the next generation of disciples will be underprepared to teach others to obey everything that Jesus commanded (Matt. 28:20).

Because of its relational focus, the pace required is variable and customized to each person. So you go as fast—or as slow—as you need to prepare your disciple to be able to make another disciple. Personally speaking, it's one of the most challenging, counter-intuitive lessons I've had to learn in transitioning from CAWKI to DMM: Go slow. In fact, to be more accurate, it's best to take speed out of the equation altogether. Obviously, the sense of urgency to see multiplication happen drives you toward getting the desired outcomes as soon as possible. But thinking of it in terms of a timeframe artificially complicates the process.

Discipleship is not a microwave process. It is the epitome of three steps forward and two steps back. It's messy; people are faulty. They make mistakes. They get discouraged and distracted. Stuff happens. Every person learns and absorbs things at different rates. Some start further along, while others start with nothing. Often those most responsive to God have hit rock bottom in their lives, so there are practical life issues (relational dysfunction, addictions, employment changes, etc.) that must be managed in addition to their spiritual growth. Still others have to unlearn certain things before they can replace it with new knowledge, insights, approaches, and practices.

> Jesus discipled twelve men (three of whom were apparently an inner circle), lived with them 24/7, eventually lost one at the end—and spent three and one-half years doing it.

New disciples will get it right, but they also will get it wrong. It's a developmental process; it's analogous to raising children, and it requires the same kind of patience and consistency as a disciple-maker. It involves a lot of practical "I-do/you-watch, you-do/I-help, you-do/I-watch" activities. These simply take time, and artificially speeding up the process will short-change it.

This can be particularly challenging in a Western context where we all have full calendars and small windows of availability. It requires discipline and dedication to the process to ensure that our disciples are being equipped.

I find it a great help to look at the model of Jesus. He discipled twelve men (three of whom were apparently an inner circle), lived with them 24/7, eventually lost one at the end—and spent three and one-half years doing it. Jesus could have easily sped up the process, perhaps by doing a few more remarkable and visible miracles. But he chose not to. He could easily have included more people with larger venues, but consistently avoided those opportunities.

Why? Only he can answer that question fully. But it seems reasonable to assume that part of the strategy was to initiate and model a disciple-making process others could and would imitate. And it's a process that simply can't be rushed.

Contrast #9 – Key Metric: Attenders vs. Capable Disciple-Makers

In my leadership and management coaching, I like to help my clients come to terms with an important principle: You hit what you aim for; so are you clear on what you're aiming for—*really* aiming for? There are several important implications to this question.

The first is simply the act of setting a goal. If you're targeting nothing, you can be confident in knowing that's exactly what you'll hit: nothing. The second is being as clear as possible on your targeted goal—which is different than an assumption, a hope, or an expectation. The third is making sure your target is the right one, which is often the most challenging step. Having the wrong target will be counterproductive, distracting, or a set up for failure. This takes wisdom, discernment, and experience; and often times faith.

Once you have a goal that's clearly defined and you're convinced it's the right one, the next step is to evaluate what you're doing to achieve it. This is where metrics come into play. How will you objectively measure your activity and your results to ensure you will reach your goal?

Legacy Ministry Metrics

As discussed in chapter 1, 'Is It Working?', attendance is the driving metric for most legacy churches (along with giving). There are a number of issues with this when it comes to making disciples and achieving disciple-making multiplication.

- Worship attendance and weekly giving are examples of "lag" metrics (outcomes that confirm—after the fact—whether or not you achieved your goal). Some churches also devote attention to "lead" metrics (activities or processes that drive the outcomes), but many don't. Without knowing what activities (lead) are driving the outcomes (lag), you're left with simply making assumptions about the outcomes you experience.[2]

- Measuring attendance (and giving) isn't directly correlated with the goal Jesus has called us to: Making disciples of all nations. The only thing the vast majority of legacy churches can definitively claim about increased worship attendance or giving per family is they had more people present in the building and those people donated more money.

- Even counting baptisms (unquestionably a relevant lag metric) only confirms how many people have professed faith in Christ; it doesn't confirm that they are equipped or active in disciple-making.

- Many churches will measure the percentage of attendees participating in other ministry programs, such as small groups, gender ministries, Sunday School, etc. While this additional level of metrics is helpful, they are still lag metrics that don't identify the activities or processes that drove them.

These issues reveal just how subjective it is to use attendance as a gauge for church health. It leaves quite a number of issues open to interpretation and it can easily devolve to varying levels of oversimplification, opinion, emotion, and misjudgment.

DMM Metrics

A healthy disciple-multiplying movement consistently monitors a handful of key lead metrics as well as some lag metrics and macro level outcomes. The specific metrics used in DMMs vary by movement. In 1Body Church's movement, we track metrics at two different levels: 1) An individual level for each person who's discipling someone else, and 2) an overall, macro level that includes all the simple churches in our network.

At the individual level, we use our Core Practices Mentor Guide to take a periodic assessment (two or three times a year) with our emerging leaders (those early in their disciple-making experience). The assessment evaluates levels of competency of our Core Practices, behavioral habits, and disciplines we consider vital to the effectiveness of disciple-making. We also use the Mentor Guide as the basis for regular coaching conversations with each leader, training them in the process to use it with the person(s) they're discipling. This allows us to gauge the leaders' progress in being a disciple as well as the effectiveness of their training with the person they are discipling.[3]

At the macro level, we monitor the health and progress of each disciple-making gathering, which we designate as either groups or home churches (groups include people in the initial stages of the disciple-making process, which then usually transition into a home church when they covenant together to function as a church).[4] The network metrics we assess for each gathering include:

- The ratio of believers to non-believers in the gathering
- The number of people in the gathering that have been baptized (total and since the group start)
- The number of people in the gathering actively discipling someone else toward starting their own group

- The number of people in the gathering involved in an accountability relationship (see *Contrast #22* on page 177)
- If the gathering is functioning as a group or a home church (Y/N)

We also monitor our network generational map, which shows how the gatherings are connected relationally with each other. This reveals the generations of discipleship groups that have been formed as disciples mentor others to start a group of their own.

By tracking some additional basic logistical data for each gathering (when the group started, where it is located, day it usually meets and who the leader is), we can also track visually where our disciple-making efforts are occurring and how they progress over time.

What's important to note in all the above metrics is we are vitally interested in measuring how effective we are in our lead metrics, the activities and processes that produce disciple-making disciples:

- The ratio of believers/non-believers reveals how much and how effectively we are interacting with people who don't yet know Jesus
- The number of baptisms reveals if our process of discipleship is leading to new professions of faith
- The number actively discipling others shows our effort toward reproducing disciples and starting new home churches
- The number of people practicing accountability reveals the commitment toward maturity in the faith
- The ratio of groups to churches reveals a deepening commitment to Christian community
- The physical location (on a map) reveals where our disciple-making efforts are—and where they are not

We are less interested in measuring lag metrics that reflect broad outcomes. For instance, we don't track the typical metrics of total attendance or giving since neither of these are drivers to discipleship multiplication. We know if we get the lead processes right, the lag metrics will come. In essence, it is the corporate equivalent to staying connected to the vine (John 15): We don't focus on the fruit, we focus on abiding with God and letting him bear the fruit through us.

By dashboarding these metrics and tracking the changes over time we are able to immediately spot which disciplines are strong and vital, as well as those that are weak and need to be strengthened. It provides visibility to know where to focus our leadership and management efforts.

> **We know if we get the lead processes right, the lag metrics will come. In essence, it is the corporate equivalent to staying connected to the vine (John 15): We don't focus on the fruit, we focus on abiding with God and letting him bear the fruit through us.**

Ultimately, the bottom line metric is the number of healthy, functioning disciple-makers (people trained and equipped to make another disciple and actively doing so). If you can only track one thing, that's the one to track; the more equipped disciple-makers you have, the more disciples you can make—by God's grace.

Contrast #10 – Ministry Application: Programmatic vs. Personal

What's the best delivery vehicle for disciple-making? How should the church orient people to the concept of being a disciple? How do we equip followers of Jesus to become disciples who can make other disciples?

The ways CAWKI and DMM answer these questions differ wildly.

Discipleship As a Participant Program
As mentioned earlier, in many cases "discipleship" in a legacy context has a more narrow meaning of teaching someone the deeper knowledge

of the Bible and the finer points of theology and doctrine. These are viewed as necessary steps in order to reach Christian maturity. Apart from this viewpoint being too narrow is the additional concern of how discipleship is sponsored and promoted in the life of the church.

My experience is that many legacy churches do not have an intentional, organized process for discipleship. For those that do, it usually takes the form of an organized program utilizing an educational format. Participants work their way through an approved curriculum with designated instructors with demonstrated knowledge and experience to facilitate the program. Often the program is run on a scheduled, seasonal ,or even a series approach.

When participants complete the program there may or may not be a next step in mind. Often there's very little, if any, opportunity to apply the learning once the program is completed. Because the program is a one-on-many setting, an ongoing mentoring relationship with the instructor may not built or maintained.

That this is an educational approach to discipleship is once again obvious. As I have already addressed: Discipleship is more than just something you know intellectually. So any program that doesn't include practice for skill development is going to fall short of equipping people to make disciples. And you run the risk of believers who have completed a program thinking they understand discipleship, yet not being able to practice it or reproduce it effectively.

But there's another aspect to a programmatic approach to discipleship that should be observed. When discipleship is a program—separate from the other programs the church offers, that only a subset of the congregation participates in—what does it say to the congregation (especially those who don't participate)? It may say a lot of things, but unquestionably it communicates that discipleship is optional to both the mission of the church and the life of a follower of Jesus.

Discipleship As a Personal Way of Life

A DMM is set up to leverage the reality that discipleship is our life; our identity as Jesus' followers. And because it's our life it doesn't need to be contained or constrained by the limitations of a scheduled program. It happens anywhere, any time. Discipleship connections can be established with the person sitting next to you on the airplane, or with the server who waits on you at the restaurant, or with your neighbor.

Discipleship is not just about knowledge, it's about surrendering our lives to Jesus and letting the Holy Spirit guide us into all righteousness. Everything we do in life is brought under the single focus of living out Jesus' teachings and lifestyle. This approach integrates life and faith, making both clear, focused and single-minded.

It's just life.

It makes for relational interactions with people, because there's no artificial agenda or timetable to maintain. Instead of answering a list of prescribed discussion questions with a group, you just communicate; you talk, and you listen to each other. Disciple-making is run on the Lord's schedule, it's not calendarized. It's people-based, not production-based. It is not segmented, but instead it holistically impacts our lives and requires—or invites—interaction well beyond a structured curriculum. It pushes away hypocrisy, because it's harder to maintain separate silos where you can be different people in different situations.

Discarding a programmatic practice of faith is one of the more subtle differences with the legacy church, but I think it's also one of the more profound. As an example, I'd like to tell you the story of the University Mall neighborhood in Tampa.

Our church was led to this neighborhood the locals call "Suitcase City." It's a poor area filled with the typical dynamics you'd find in a desperate urban neighborhood, like crime, drugs, prostitution, and gang activity. It's also a center for refugee housing, which means there are numerous nationalities, languages, and religions—complicating the mistrust, skepticism, and isolation so thick one could cut it with a knife.

Lots of churches and organizations over the years have come into the neighborhood to "help." But their programmatic efforts did more damage than good. Churches came, preached about Jesus' love, spent some money … and left. To the residents this felt self-serving and insulting, as if the churches needed to check off a community service project box on their to-do list.

> When discipleship is a program—separate from the other programs the church offers, that only a subset of the congregation participates in—what does it say to the congregation (especially those who don't participate)?

Because our approach is relational discipleship, we've had a number of people in our church move into the neighborhood. It took several years of living with people and patiently demonstrating love in a discipleship context to earn their trust.

We have a number of initiatives we're partnering with members of the community, like a parent-directed homeschool co-op, a community garden and starting a business that will bring stability and income opportunities. But none of it would have happened if the relationships weren't there first.

The message of the love of Christ needs a relationship bridge to walk across. Christianity is an incarnational faith: In the same way Jesus came to earth to show us the love of the Father, we must "go" to people to relate with them on their turf and in their lives to demonstrate the gospel and call them to faith in Christ.

Can this be accomplished in a programmed approach? Maybe. But all too often the program is more important than the people in it. If relationship is where we want to end up, why not just start there?

Contrast #11 – Primary Meeting Structure: Congregation vs. Small Group

The church's primary gatherings reveal its priorities. The primary gathering for CAWKI is a congregational service, typically (though not always) on Sunday morning in a designated venue. The primary gathering in a DMM is a small gathering of people that meet almost anywhere: homes, coffee houses, businesses, parks, etc. Let's evaluate each gathering from the perspective of multiplying disciples.

Large and Complex
CAWKI's congregational service involves a large number of people (with little-to-no interaction), requires a large and specially-equipped space, is tightly programmed and requires a significant investment of time and energy to coordinate and conduct (usually by paid staff and dedicated volunteers who are serving in some capacity). It's main emphasis is typically worship and teaching. It involves (usually) a worship component, whether it's a band, choir, or chorus. Contemporary services also utilize video which must be edited and prepared. And, of course, the sermon must be prepared and taught by a qualified teacher.

The worship gathering is a one-on-many, passive experience (see *Contrast #21* on page 172) that likely includes people with a wide variety of spiritual maturity and commitment levels (see *Contrast #17* on page 156). This format is largely impersonal. By this I don't mean cold or unwelcoming; the logistics of the gathering simply do not provide a way to make it interactive, relational, and relevant at an individual level.

To accommodate for this impersonal dynamic, many legacy churches also sponsor small group gatherings as a supplement. These groups are helpful, but joining a small group requires another time commitment. Many of the legacy church's attenders simply don't or can't participate.

Another gathering format growing in popularity is what I'll generically call the house church approach. This is a kind of hybrid gathering that miniaturizes and simplifies CAWKI's worship service by relocating it to the more casual, relational, and intimate setting of a house. This format does provide for more personal interaction and potentially stronger relationships and is easier to reproduce than a large legacy gathering.

However, these types of house churches may not be set up with intentional multiplication in mind. House churches that operate with a "come" mentality will not ultimately multiply. Just because it meets in a house doesn't ensure church participants will "go" to those who need to hear the gospel.

Typically, the primary limiting factor for reproduction in this type of house church approach is the need for qualified leaders. Each house church must be pastored by an authorized and trained leader (usually teacher)—the same leadership challenge that larger legacy churches face. Identifying and apprenticing these leaders takes significant time and effort because of the role they play.

Small and Simple

The primary gathering in a DMM is a small group. In our particular branch of DMM we call this gathering either groups or home churches (if the group has reached a level of commitment to function as a church). The format we use is called ⅓rds discussion; other DMM streams call them discovery Bible study (DBS). "⅓rds" describes how the discussion is broken into three parts:

    1. Look back (to review since the last meeting),

2. Look up (to see what God wants to reveal to us through the Bible), and

3. Look forward (to focus on how we will obey what God has revealed).

A ⅓rds group (whether or not it's functioning as a church) involves a small number of people, doesn't require a trained, authorized pastor/teacher, can meet anywhere/anytime, has a very simple, consistent order, and everyone participates in the discussion. In fact, everyone takes turns facilitating the discussion since every disciple needs to be prepared to mentor a new disciple on how to lead a ⅓rds discussion. It can be done in as little as thirty minutes or as long as four to five hours around a communal meal.

The ⅓rds group's main emphases are hearing from God and creating mutual accountability around 1) how to obey the Scripture, 2) who to share it with, and 3) how you will use it to train others. The resulting dynamics are transparent discovery, hearing from God, and creating mutual commitments around what and how to follow his leading. Added to this is the missional aspect of reaching out to those who don't know Christ. Each meeting involves praying for the people each member will share the topics of discussion with and discussing how to support each other throughout the week.

The 3/3ʳᵈˢ or DBS formats don't require additional effort to insert a disciple-making focus. In fact, the only time this format is ineffective is when the members don't want to participate in discipleship—which is revealing.

This group approach also includes opportunities for the "one another's" to occur—all the 58 commands from the New Testament about how we are to interact with one another: bear one another's burdens, love one another, forgive one another, etc. As participants interact,

things like individual needs, hurts, celebrations, and personal victo-
ries are revealed, as well as opportunities for the group to serve others
outside of the group.

All of these elements create a gathering that is easily repeatable
and adaptable, and fits virtually everyone from of all levels of spiritual
interest and maturity. It also incites discipleship and multiplication.
The ⅓rds or DBS formats don't require additional effort to insert a
disciple-making focus. In fact, the only time this format is ineffective is
when the members don't want to participate in discipleship—which
is revealing.

7

How the Church Is Led and Developed

As for the future, your task is not to foresee it, but to enable it.

—Antoine de Saint Exupéry

As the quality of the church's leadership goes, so goes the church. This has been true throughout time and across all cultures. When God's people are led well with integrity, the church flourishes. When not, the church struggles. How leaders are recognized, developed, equipped, established, and empowered may be the single greatest thing we (as God's people) can do to set up the church to effectively accomplish the Great Commission.

The function and development of leadership in a DMM is vastly different than in a CAWKI ministry model, making this series of contrasts perhaps the most challenging to compare.

┌─ **Church Leadership Contrasts** ─────────────────────┐

12 – Leadership:

Professional Clergy vs. Bivocational Leader

13 – Maturity Gauge:

Knowledge vs. Christlikeness

14 – The Equipping Gifts:

Shepherds & Teachers vs. APEST

15 – Management Approach:

Control vs. Release

└──┘

Contrast #12 – Leadership:
Professional Clergy vs. Bivocational Leader

Discussing a diverse and multifaceted discipline like leadership is a challenge. There are so many perspectives on what it is, the role it plays, and how it functions. Given that we're evaluating ministry leadership that will contribute toward discipleship multiplication, it can be even more challenging. It may be helpful to clarify a definition of ministry leadership to orient us toward a common understanding.

I would define leadership in simple terms as the act of inspiring and motivating others to achieve an envisioned outcome. I also recommend viewing leadership simply as the art of exercising influence. John Maxwell was the first person I know to associate the concepts, though I'm sure there are others who also have. Though it has lately been associated more with C-suite, corporate leadership, influence is still one of the best descriptions of leadership because it most accurately describes the nature of what leadership accomplishes—apart from style or personality. Effective leadership thinks and operates at the level of change: It recognizes what needs to change, and it drives those changes until the goal is achieved.

Influence is still one of the best descriptions of leadership because it most accurately describes the nature of what leadership accomplishes.

Leadership in the Church
Since the words "lead," "leader," and "leadership" are not in the original texts of the Bible, it's important that we recognize several functions and practices called out in the Scriptures to use as a foundation for our modern terminology.

Overseeing (1 Timothy 3:2)

The Greek word *episkopeo* is used to define the practice of leaders in the church (see 1 Pet. 5:2). It has typically been translated as "overseeing," and means to watch over, inspect, look after, and to care for in a way that mimics God's loving care and concern for his people. In the early church—as a network organization—the responsibility to oversee was distributed broadly across the church. While the activity of overseeing was (appropriately) applied to senior leaders with a specific title like elders, it was not limited to the individuals with those titles (see Heb. 12:15). Said another way: In the New Testament, elders (*presbuteros*) are overseers (*episkopos*), but overseers are not exclusively elders.[1]

Another Greek word, *proistemi*, describes the activity of those who oversee (*episkopeo*). Literally translated it means *to stand before*, which carries the sense of being able to direct and positively impact by way of example. It has been translated into English in various terms, such as "lead" or "rule" (Rom. 12:8), "have charge over," "care for," "[be] over," "preside over," (1 Thess. 5:12), "manage," "rule" (1 Tim. 3:4–5, 3:12), and "rule," "direct" and "provide effective leadership" (1 Tim. 5:17).[2]

Equipping (Ephesians 4:12)

Leadership in the church is to be applied toward the people of God for the purpose of building up both individuals and the church, with the desired outcome of maturity in Christ. The five equipping gifts listed in this passage—apostles, prophets, evangelists, shepherds, and teachers (APEST)—are best seen as the necessary types of influence for the church to achieve maturity and stability (see *Contrast #14* on page 139 for more discussion).

Exercising Leadership As a Gift (Romans 12:8)

Some believers are gifted specifically as leaders, which expands on the use of the APEST gifts from Ephesians 4:12. Pairing the two passages together places a leadership emphasis on equipping others. In short, if a believer has the capacity to influence others toward maturity then that believer should seize opportunities to influence with all diligence as a "spiritual service of worship" (Rom. 12:2, NASB).

By implication, it's self-evident that the organization of the church should provide opportunities for those with the gift of leadership to exercise it to their fullest. In other words, the church should be about the business of recognizing and delegating leadership authority and responsibility.

Serving (John 13:3–17)

This is perhaps the most significant component of ministry leadership. Church leaders should intentionally position themselves to serve the needs of those they lead, and do so as an example to others (see 1 Pet. 5:3 and the emphasis on leading by example). That Jesus specifically demonstrated this through the seminal act of washing his disciples' feet (including those of his betrayer) makes serving an unmistakable priority for effective ministry leadership. Perhaps even more compelling is that Jesus' example was not a command, but a recommendation. He could have issued an imperative for the disciples to practice servant leadership, but rather simply predicted blessing if they did. Influencing through the servant role is a volitional choice each leader must make.

> That Jesus specifically demonstrated [positioning himself as a servant] through the seminal act of washing his disciples' feet (including those of his betrayer) makes serving an unmistakable priority for effective ministry leadership.

This also means actively abandoning the use of positional authority (Matt. 20:26, Mark 10:43). Jesus indicated that the "rulers" of the Gentiles (Greek *archon*, those who were first in positional authority)[3] exercised dominion by "lording" their authority over others. Jesus rejected this approach in favor of a being a servant: Instead of vying to be first or foremost, leaders should make every effort to be last or lowest in order to elevate those they serve through the exercise of their leadership.

As an example, consider Paul's recollection of his leadership approach to the Thessalonian church:

> "You know we never used flattery, nor did we put on a mask to cover up greed—God is our witness. We were not looking for praise from people, not from you or anyone else, even though as apostles of Christ we could have asserted our authority. Instead, we were like young children among you." (1 Thess. 2:5–7)

We can use these four emphases of leadership influence—overseeing, equipping, exercising leadership as a gift and serving—to evaluate and contrast how leaders function in both the legacy and the DMM ministry models.

CAWKI and Leadership

It is challenging to relationally influence others in a CAWKI organizational model. The hierarchical structure discussed in chapter 7—along with the clergy-laity divide—automatically places leaders above others and bestows positional authority on them. By default, leaders in the legacy church have to give extra effort to avoid the very approach Jesus asked us not to adopt.

Leadership is narrowly distributed across the typical legacy organization, residing in a few ordained ministers in specialized, programmed roles. These few then face an overwhelmingly large span of care. Their influence is centralized, restricted, and limited to one-on-many mechanisms (congregational preaching, communication meetings, social media posts, newsletters, etc.). Overseeing is limited to managing compliance and monitoring high-level metrics (see *Contrast #9* on page 115 and see *Contrast #14* on page 139).

Compounding this is the reality that the legacy organizational model limits the number of leadership opportunities and makes it hard to develop other leaders. Most of the leadership opportunities are paid-staff, program-oriented roles, which restricts the number of qualified leadership candidates.

The equipping process for professional, ordained clergy is another restrictive barrier. The educational process is expensive, time-consuming, and narrowly focused (e.g., teaching). And because the seminaries and Bible colleges typically support specific denominations or traditions, the preparation process reinforces and prolongs the current division of the church we see in the West.

All these issues demonstrate why the approach to leadership in a CAWKI environment blocks discipleship multiplication. The entire process is complex and weighty. It takes an enormous amount of time, expense, and effort to produce a leader who then spends most of his/her time in a one-to-many programmed role with limited access to influence people directly. This is not the fault of the churches or pastors who want to see the church prosper and grow disciples. The fault lies in a model that simply restricts it from happening.

Leadership in a DMM environment
Leadership is baked into the disciple-making process from the very first conversation. The priorities of caring and looking out for your

132

disciple are part of the discipleship DNA and are immediately practiced, regardless of the maturity level of the disciple-maker.

As disciple-makers grow in their faith, their effectiveness to oversee grows with it. Influence is developed relationally, through an organic, supportive, mentoring relationship with the person being discipled. The one-on-one (or one-on-few) encounters allow for a natural and holistic relationship experience. Trust is earned over time and authority is validated through demonstrated mentoring opportunities.

Leaders are developed organically, and their giftedness, faithfulness, wisdom, and maturity are confirmed as they disciple others. The scale of their influence grows as more disciple generations are born. The more strongly-gifted leaders become evident, and their influence gradually expands to the broader network rather than just their own discipleship generations.

The discipleship process is naturally both developmental and delegation-intensive from a leadership perspective. A disciple-maker's intent is to give authority and responsibility away to the new disciple early and often. As each aspect of being a disciple is practiced and mastered, the disciple gains both confidence and a higher sense of calling.

By default, leaders in the legacy church have to give extra effort to avoid the very approach Jesus asked us not to adopt.

It may be best to think of leadership development in a disciple-making context as an apprenticeship process—think Yoda and Luke Skywalker. The goal is to equip a new generation of practitioners through modeling and on-the-job training experiences until they can perform on their own. The "master" can't control, manipulate, or force the "apprentice" to develop or make their decisions for them, but can show them the way and influence them. The skilled disciple-making practitioner uses multiple methods to pass along disciple-making tools: motivation, challenge, information, inspiration, correction, demonstration, care, and concern, etc. But ultimately, the

133

disciple is following their own calling and motivation to reach a level of competency. Once achieved, they are able to complete the process with someone else.

Disciple-making supports servant leadership. It's easier to take the focus off yourself when your goal is to equip another person. In a network organization there's no positional reputation to maintain. Simply said, the more of yourself you give away, the more effective you are and the more fruitful your ministry becomes.

Spiritual authority in a disciple-multiplying movement isn't based on the positional level you occupy. Instead, authority is relationally conferred from Christ himself. "All authority in heaven and on earth has been given to me," Jesus said in Matthew 28:19. His authority— delegated to him by the Father—is the basis on which the disciple-making process functions. His disciples were to proceed not on their own merited or organizational authority, but on that of the Savior (see, for example, Acts 4:5–12).

Jesus then book-ends the Great Commission with the promise, "And I am with you always, even to the end of the age"—implying that the conferred authority was not just for his eleven disciples but to the entire disciple-multiplying movement they would initiate. Jesus is both our example and our source of authority. All disciple-makers follow him as they model his life and commands and equip their disciples accordingly.

Practical Aspects of Bivocational Leadership
When it comes to the question of staffing leaders in a DMM organization, we should consider bivocational leadership: leaders that are self-supported or working in the marketplace to earn income. Because disciple-making is more relational than programmatic, bivocational leaders can utilize their time efficiently and effectively,

meeting with people one-on-one while maintaining a full- or part-time job.

In addition to many of the issues identified above, there are a number of practical advantages to bivocational leadership in the disciple-multiplying movement church:

- It engages leaders who have other practical skills (HR, management, accounting, sales, project management, training, etc.). This broad base of skills and experience brings a strength of diversity into the leadership of the church, making it more balanced and well-rounded.
- It frees up the church from the burden of paying staff salaries.
- The ministry isn't dependent on the harvest for financial support.
- It eliminates putting leaders in the position of being obligated to someone else's giving and the appearance of "peddling the gospel for personal profit" (2 Cor. 2:17).
- It doesn't require as many leaders with specialized programmatic experience, training, or qualifications.
- It puts leaders out among the harvest of people who need to know about Jesus, allowing even their employment to become part of the "go" mechanism of discipleship.

The issue of professional clergy vs. bivocational leadership is not a black-and-white, hard-and-fast rule. A DMM strategy doesn't dismiss the use of full-time paid clergy roles, nor does it demand that every leader be bivocational. It merely gives the church more options to consider as it determines how best to meet the leadership demands of the organization.

Elders in the Church
The application of elders in a DMM approach is a regular question we receive from Western church leaders. Establishing elders in a DMM

church network is considered an important step toward the proper and healthy functioning of the church. They play an extremely important role, just as they do in a legacy church approach.

The most common point of confusion centers on how elders effectively oversee the distributed groups. It's obviously impractical—if not impossible—to have an elder in each and every simple church in the network. But it can be a challenge to get your mind around an alternative because the CAWKI paradigm is so dominant.

> It may be best to think of leadership development in a disciple-making context as an apprenticeship process—think Yoda and Luke Skywalker.

It may be helpful to remember that church is the people, not the building or the organization. In a DMM church the people gather in a variety of simple churches in a given city or region. Just as Paul directed Titus to "appoint elders in each city" (Titus 1:5), the footprint in which the elders function is the city/region where the collection of simple churches reside. As the number of churches grows, the number of elders can grow accordingly as wisdom permits and the need dictates.

Contrast #13 – Maturity Gauge: Knowledge vs. Christlikeness

This topic is closely related to *Contrast #7 – Primary Method: Teaching vs. Training* (page 108). The point of this contrast is to consider what both CAWKI and DMM methods view, measure, and celebrate as outcomes.

Knowing About God
When it comes to gauging the effectiveness of a teaching-oriented ministry, the default action is to measure the knowledge gained.

136

Consider how the legacy church models, incentivizes, rewards, and celebrates the acquisition of knowledge—both overtly and indirectly.

The subtle danger with a teaching-centric method is in perpetuating a belief that knowledge of Scripture and doctrine is the measure of maturity. This is the essence of James' warning to his readers: Knowledge alone is not an adequate, saving faith in Christ. Even demons have knowledge that there is one God.[4] This is also one of the issues Paul wrestled with the Corinthian church, who had an elevated and skewed view of their own spiritual maturity. "We know that 'We all possess knowledge,'" Paul exhorted. "But knowledge puffs up while love builds up. Those who think they know something do not yet know as they ought to know. But whoever loves God is known by God" (1 Cor. 8:1–3).

The challenge comes in realizing the enormous barrier between knowing about God and knowing God. It is relatively easy to learn about God. Knowledge acquisition is easy to measure and validate which gives us a sense of accomplishment. But it requires much more time and disciplined effort to practice and apply learning; only then does learning become wisdom.

I don't want to paint this with too broad a brush—I realize many legacy churches actively challenge people to move beyond intellectualizing faith in Christ, and they are to be commended. But the fact remains we have a systemic approach to faith that centers on teaching. Knowledge alone doesn't transform our lives to be more like Christ; intellectual assent is not an exercise of faith.

Should we operate on the assumption that knowledge is the essential ingredient behind following Jesus (as mentioned in *Contrast #7 – Primary Method: Teaching vs. Training* [page 108])? How much knowledge do we need to be able to love God wholly and love others as ourselves? How much teaching is necessary to equip someone to make another disciple? When do we address the problem of acquiring new knowledge before practicing the knowledge we already have?

Knowing God

In DMM, it is immediately apparent to all involved—even to those who haven't yet professed faith in Christ—that those who are most mature are the ones who look most like Jesus. This is held up as both the goal of the faith and the natural outcome of practicing it.

Those who most look like Jesus may or may not have deep biblical and theological knowledge, but they are the best models to follow. They demonstrate the fruits of the Spirit most vividly—peace, love, joy, patience, kindness, goodness, faithfulness, gentleness, and self-control. They are the ones who do only what the Holy Spirit directs them to do. They are the ones least impacted by the world or their flesh. They are the ones who have a deeper evidence of abiding with Christ. And—though I offer this cautiously—the fruit of their lives is often evident: They make better disciples.

Like the legacy approach, DMM also encourages biblical knowledge but with a different emphasis. In the West, we tend to view knowledge as intellectual, cognitive understanding. But the perspective on knowledge in disciple-making is more about understanding to a complete degree. For example, the Greek word most broadly used in the New Testament for knowing (*ginosko*) was even used to translate the act of sexual intercourse (as in Joseph had not "known" his wife Mary, who was a virgin, when their child Jesus was born in Matt. 1:25). To "know" meant to know completely, at every level: experientially and intellectually.[5]

We come to recognize, hear, and understand the voice of our Shepherd by actively listening, trusting, and applying what he tells us. We learn of God's faithfulness by actively stepping into the unknown and trusting him even though the way forward is not clear. We can only truly understand what it means to be encouraged or comforted by the Holy Spirit when we are in difficult situations. These things can't be known only at an intellectual level.

Dmm is designed to immediately practice any insight gained from reading the Scriptures, with a view toward transformation into Christlikeness. We apply supportive and mutual, loving accountability around this process as a part of faith training at both the individual and group levels. The result is a life typified by Christ-like surrender to and alignment with God, an abiding trust in him, obedience to Jesus through the leading of the Holy Spirit, and the commitment to shape these qualities in others. This positions us for a fruitful outcome.

I want to be realistic and fair: I'm not implying that cawki won't produce mature believers who look like Jesus. Neither am I implying that every believer in a dmm ministry is mature.

I am, however, clarifying that the dmm ministry model offers an advantage. Cawki must go the extra mile and apply more diligence to ensure people move beyond the mere acquisition of knowledge as a gauge of spiritual maturity. Dmm more clearly, quickly, and repeatedly describes faith maturity as Christ-likeness. It is this clarity which contributes to the process of multiplication.

Contrast #14 – The Equipping Gifts: Shepherds & Teachers vs. APEST

As mentioned in *Contrast #12 – Leadership: Professional Clergy vs. Bivocational Leader* (page 128), APEST is an acronym for the five equipping gifts listed in Ephesians 4:11: apostles, prophets, evangelists, shepherds/pastors, and teachers. The context of the passage makes it clear that these are gifts given individually to all believers, according to the grace of Christ. These are not titles or positions as much as they are roles and functions. The gifts are individuals with particular spiritual insight and ability working together collaboratively. Each individually and all five collectively are necessary for the building up of the church to maturity.

Here's a brief explanation of each gift and the particular abilities it brings:

- Apostles break new ground and expand the church beyond its current footprint, and are effective at reaching its culture with the gospel and breaching the barriers of the gospel in creative ways.[6]
- Prophets recognize the negative and destructive influences facing the church. They are motivated to help the church maintain a level of purity and accuracy, to remain true to its mission, and embrace truth as its guidance. Prophets highlight the reality and impact of errors and shortcomings.
- Evangelists actively pronounce the good news of the gospel, announce the presence of Christ's kingdom, and lead others to full and complete trust in Christ as their Lord and Savior.
- Shepherds/Pastors promote mutual care and encouragement for each other, bearing each other's burdens, being kind and compassionate toward each other.
- Teachers help others understand the truths of God and the Scriptures, and equip the people of God to be able to recognize and reject fallacious and erroneous views of God.

There is a distinct difference between how the equipping gifts are developed and utilized in CAWKI and in a DMM setting.

140

How CAWKI Equips

Teachers rose to prominence in the early centuries of the church (as noted in chapter 3) exercising enormous influence in defining orthodox belief. Sacerdotalism elevated the authoritative role of the clergy, which was then further cemented by the teaching emphasis of the senior pastor in the Reformation church. All this cast the die for what we now see as pastoral roles for the church in the West, which has been reinforced by the establishment of formal Christian education and seminary training.

> The legacy church has become so specialized in its teaching and shepherding focus that a new organizational category was created: para-church ministries.

The recognition and esteem of the shepherding/ pastoring and teaching gifts have been elevated over the church's history, while the apostles and prophets have been marginalized. This results in a church that is overwhelmingly biased toward teaching and shepherding. These are now both the primary expression of the church and the primary equipping process for future CAWKI leaders.

The legacy church has become so specialized in its teaching and shepherding focus that a new organizational category was created: para-church ministries. The result is that church has effectively outsourced many efforts that, from a New Testament perspective, were considered ecclesiastical responsibilities—if not missional opportunities. Things like cross-cultural missions, care for the persecuted church, discipleship, care for the homeless, elderly, or single-parents, or a host of other social ministry functions. The church, properly positioned, could take the lead in such areas. But the way it is currently structured and focused simply prohibits effective, sustainable outreach into these areas of ministry—where the fields are white for harvest.

How DMM Equips

DMM emphasizes the missional call of each believer. Every person that follows Jesus is a potential leader of a stream of discipleship movement. As such, each believer is called to apply himself/herself as God has equipped them and as the Holy Spirit leads. This means all five of the APEST equipping gifts will be deployed, ensuring the ministry efforts of the church will be balanced and strong.[7]

Think of it this way: A church that is not using all five gifts in a complementary, collaborative way simply will not be a stable, growing, impactful, relevant, caring, and compassionate church.

- *A Church that is not* ... breaking new ground and expanding beyond its current footprint, and is not effective at creatively reaching its culture with the gospel and breaching the barriers of the gospel
  - *Will eventually* ... be static and stuck in forms that are ineffective when facing significant changes; unable to bridge across cultures or successful transition into new eras
    - *Unless this gift is used*: Apostles
- *A Church That is Not* ... recognizing the negative and destructive influences it faces, not striving to maintain a level of purity and accuracy, not remaining true to its mission, not embracing
  - *Will eventually* ... Become weak, splintered, and disunified, lose the grand view of the holiness of God and ultimately drift off its mission
    - *Unless this gift is used*: Prophets
- *A Church that is not* ... Actively pronouncing the good news of the gospel of Jesus Christ, announcing the presence of his kingdom, and leading others to full and complete trust in Christ as

142

their Lord and Savior truth, not willing to face the reality of its errors and shortcomings

- o *Will eventually* ...Become ingrown and lifeless, move toward social justice issues as a replacement for a faith relationship with Jesus, and die a slow death
  - • *Unless this gift is used:* Evangelists
- • *A Church that is not* ... Modeling the love of Jesus, caring for each other, bearing each other's burdens, etc., being intentionally kind and compassionate
  - o *Will eventually* ... Become a closed community, characterized by judgmental, unforgiving, and legalistic attitudes
    - • *Unless this gift is used:* Shepherds
- • *A Church that is not* ... Teaching the truths of God and the Scriptures, rejecting fallacious and erroneous views of God
  - o *Will eventually* ... Embrace worldly philosophy and lies that drive it toward a human-centered religion that is Christian in name-only
    - • *Unless this gift is used:* Teachers

The church needs all five of the APEST gifts present and active in the equipping process to be effective. If the gifts aren't in balance, it will not be a church where disciples are trained and equipped—and the fruit of discipleship multiplication simply won't occur.

If This Gift is Dominant...	The Church Will Eventually Be...
Apostles	Autocratic and challenge-driven in its leadership, chaotic in its management approach, heavily entrepreneurial with few sustainable and repeatable processes, lots of hurt people
Prophets	One-dimensional, issue-driven, factious, exclusive, judgmental, and legalistic, rule-based, activist, and potentially hyper-spiritual
Evangelists	Narrow-minded, shallow, lacking long-term transformation and growth to maturity, where the focus is on the message of salvation and not on sanctification or development, unable to endure persecution and suffering
Shepherds	Closed and internalized, non-missional, lacking willingness to embrace significant and necessary change, overly concerned for safety and security, co-dependent on pastoral leadership
Teachers	Dogmatic, educational, knowledge-heavy with an intellectual approach to faith, over-emphasizing the authority of the Bible while under-emphasizing the authority of the Holy Spirit

It may be helpful to think about applying or deploying the APEST gifts in a general sequence—especially when the church is making inroads into new areas. We illustrate this by what we called the Four Fields diagram (see Figure 1). The "fields" are not physical locations, but different types of effort and emphases in disciple-making. This is not a hard-and-fast rule, but a general, cyclical pattern that leverages the strengths of each of the five APEST gifts to equip and disciple others.

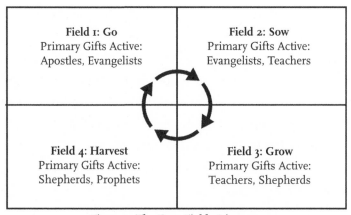

Figure 1: The Four Fields Diagram

Often new efforts are most effective when they're led by apostles and evangelists in identifying and initiating disciple-making in a new area, culture, or neighborhood. This is Field #1: Go. Then the gospel of the kingdom is announced by evangelists and teachers who establish relationships with key individuals in Field #2: Sow. Next, the teachers and shepherds take the lion's share of the effort in Field #3: Grow, as individuals come to faith, groups are formed and relationships are deepened. Finally, the shepherds and prophets take the lead in Field #4: Harvest, moving people toward following the leading of the Holy Spirit, realizing their calling, and preparing them to take part in the next round of missional disciple-making.

The entire cycle should be seen as a process of identifying believers' APEST giftedness and equipping them to leverage their gifts as they lead. Over time, each believer's gifts are exercised, recognized, confirmed, authorized, trained, developed, and affirmed. In a DMM setting, believers are immediately and constantly practicing and strengthening their gifts in the context of a collaborative, disciple-making community. Leaders and mentors are consistently delegating both opportunity and authority to their disciples to practice their gifts.

This process contributes to multiplication as believers are constantly funneled into active ministry. It creates an environment of rapid and missional leadership development that looks a lot more like the apprenticing process described in *Contrast #12* on page 128 than an educationally-driven process. Emerging leaders learn how to lead others by observing how mentors lead and then by practicing it themselves, using their equipping gifts in a mutually submissive and collaborative approach. As a result the church is built up into maturity.

Contrast #15 – Management Approach: Control vs. Release

The word "control" in our modern context comes loaded with negative associations. Let me assure you for the purposes of this contrast I mean to use "control" in a neutral sense. "Control" means to exercise restraint of direction over; to command. It also means to regulate, hold in check, or to curb.

Control is one option available to church leaders when it comes to managing the affairs and the people in the church. The other is release, the opposite of control: To avoid restraint or command over people; to intentionally minimize regulation or holding in check. Of course, it should be noted that both "control" and "release" should be seen in general terms. "Control" does not imply absolute domination, and neither does "release" imply absolute freedom from restraint.

Both control and release describe general management approaches to answer the question: How should we oversee the church and its ministry? It is a vitally important question that has drastic implications on multiplying disciple-making.

Control

One of the realities of the legacy church's management approach is the tendency for control. I see five major contributing factors to this. The first is the pattern of church governance set down in the 300s and beyond. As church leadership became centralized under the authority of the bishops in the major cities throughout the empire, it became increasingly authoritative in dealing with major questions such as orthodoxy and doctrinal issues. The church also increasingly aligned itself with the empirical governance of Rome which introduced a political emphasis into managing church affairs. Those in the minority on major issues were often marginalized, shunned, and at times excommunicated. The result set a precedent for a controlling approach to governing that the church has had a difficult time shedding.

The second factor stems from differentiation being our organizing principle (see *Contrast #3* on page 93). When we elevate a set of beliefs, traditions, or practices to be the reason we organize and separate from other fellowships, defending this set of beliefs becomes a priority. We have to expend energies to ensure others agree with, comply with, and support those beliefs.

A third contributing factor is the result of not having a diversity of the APEST gifts present in CAWKI today. As I discussed in *Contrast #14 – The Equipping Gifts: Shepherds & Teachers vs. APEST (page 139)*, the legacy church in the West today is primarily led by shepherds and teachers. The strengths of these two gifts is their ability to bring order, consistency, and a systemic, structured approach to the practice of the faith. With that ability also comes a natural tendency to control to maintain the structure. When the other gifts are not present—particularly apostles and evangelists—in a leadership capacity, the organization will naturally tend toward control as an operating process.

A fourth is a result of the centralized hierarchical leadership struc-ture (see *Contrast #4* on page 97). A centralized leadership also leans toward control as its mode of operation, rather than disseminating leadership responsibility and authority.

The final contributing factor is the most uncomfortable. Christians in the West like to be in control because this is the way of our world. Our culture and worldview hold self-determination in high esteem. To not be in control is to be perceived as being out of control; imprudent, failing to plan and execute responsibly. To make matters worse, to surrender control to someone else is seen as weakness, vulnerability, and ultimately failure. Frankly, in the West—and especially in the U.S.—we are simply more comfortable when we're exercising control.

Model, Train, and Release
DMM's management approach is to release rather than control. The mindset is to prepare people to follow the direction of the Holy Spirit at the very beginning of the discipleship process. DMM emphasizes training and equipping people to hear and trust his voice, to expect answers to prayers, to obey God's voice from the pages of the Bible, and to avoid an over-dependency on human understanding.

As people practice being controlled by the Holy Spirit, hearing his subtle promptings, and listening for his small, still voice, their faith and trust in God's control over their lives and their ministry grows and strengthens. They also become more disciplined and capable at teaching others how to follow God's direction.

It's common for people who come from legacy ministry practices to experience much deeper and closer connection to God as they begin practicing DMM. I've heard comments like, "I pray differently now," "I never sensed God was leading me personally before," and "I never realized God wanted to speak directly to me, and that I could know it was him." In cases like this, they are learning to depend directly and personally on the Holy Spirit instead of depending on the church's programming.

DMM is predicated on the belief that God is working ahead of us. God is sovereignly arranging for personal connections and conversations to occur. God is working in people and in areas we aren't aware of, and often in ways we wouldn't choose or believe are possible. If we were to use our human-centered abilities we would limit the expanse of the gospel.

In the West—and especially in the U.S.—we are simply more comfortable when we're exercising control.

The reality in the gospel and the New Testament church is that God is the only one in control of the church. It is the Holy Spirit who leads and directs us, as well as convicting the world of sin and revealing spiritual truth to unspiritual minds. We must either wholeheartedly believe this truth or choose instead to give it only token affirmation. I confess this is challenging to say, but to the degree we try to control the ministry of the church we are failing to surrender control to the Holy Spirit, which at some level is a lack of trust in him.

8 How the Church Engages with People

If you want to go fast, go alone.
If you want to go far, go together.

—African Proverb

The organization and ministry of the local church will engage with individuals both inside and outside the church. Both the CAWKI and DMM models have distinct frames of reference that define how that interaction takes place and the motives behind it.

There are five contrasts to consider when it comes to how the organization of church engages with individuals:

```
┌─ People Engagement Contrasts ─────────────────────┐
│                                                    │
│  16 – Invitation:                                  │
│            Appeal vs. Call                         │
│  17 – Onboarding:                                  │
│            Visitor vs. Sponsored Connection        │
│  18 – Converts' Cultural Impact:                   │
│            Extraction vs. Infusion                 │
│  19 – Membership Requirements:                     │
│            Compliance vs. Obedience                │
│  20 – Maturity Mindset:                            │
│            Externally Fed vs. Self-Fed             │
│                                                    │
└────────────────────────────────────────────────────┘
```

Contrast #16 – Invitation: Appeal vs. Call

In his popular book *Drive: The Surprising Truth About What Motivates Us*, author Dan Pink identifies three things that must be in place for people to have elevated and sustained levels of intrinsic motivation. Intrinsic motivation (as opposed to external sources of motivation like other people, "carrot-and-stick" incentives, etc.) must be in place for people to continue to engage, to push through setbacks and challenges, and to sacrifice in order to meet a goal. Intrinsic motivation is a key factor in high-performance and task achievement. Those three elements are:

1. Autonomy (the opportunity to direct our lives/work),
2. Mastery (the opportunity to get better at something that matters), and
3. Purpose (the opportunity to apply ourselves in the service of something bigger than ourselves).[1]

The third element—purpose—is a key factor in evaluating the church's effectiveness at making disciples that can make disciples.

The Appeal

The legacy ministry approach is set up to appeal to people and their self-interests or affinity. This is one of the outcomes of a "come" orientation to the world (see *Contrast #2* on page 91), as well as organizing around differentiation (see *Contrast #3* on page 93). With all the best of intentions, the church is marketing itself and its services to people who are seeking a church with a certain profile in mind. The church's hope is that people will be attracted and interested enough to visit.

The appeal is centered on one or more levels, like belief, denominational affiliation, life-stage, social perspective, types of services offered, worship style, etc. This branding-marketing effort is the same process we see in the consumer marketplace, where the goal is to gain as much market share with potential buyers as possible.

In a capitalistic, consumer-driven process it's important to remember that the customer is ultimately in charge—a perspective virtually all successful product or service companies will affirm. That's why companies have customer service branches: to confirm the "needs" of their customers and to adjust or improve their product or service to fit those needs so they will continue to buy more as well as provide positive reviews so others will buy.

This approach positions the church as a provider of services to the prospective new attender. It creates an expectation that the church should "feed me" or "meet my/my family's needs."

This approach positions the church as a provider of services to the prospective new attender. It creates an expectation that the church should "feed me" or "meet my/my family's needs." The resulting response from the church's perspective is to make the point of entry as broad as possible with little—and ideally no—required commitment.

Consider the outcome of having such a broad range of engagement and commitment levels of the people attending. The church must continue to expend a great deal of energy and money simply to maintain the appeal. And it is very difficult to discern their true level of interest when they are immersed in the anonymity of a large gathering.

Once people begin attending regularly, the church then moves toward raising the bar on commitment. The intention is to compel them to higher levels of service, to give more, to join the church in membership, to participate in a Bible study, small group, or Sunday School, etc. This creates a subtle but awkward tension between appealing to them as customers and challenging them to submit to God's calling for their lives.

The Call to Be a Disciple (-Maker)

In contrast with appealing at the level of self-interest, a disciple-multiplying movement approach invites people to a calling: Join a movement that will change the world forever—and in fact has already begun. It's a lifelong commitment with a high bar for entry: You must be willing to give up the life you know in the promise that God will give you a new one. And this commitment takes priority over everything else in your life; or perhaps better said, this commitment informs everything else in your life.

This approach reminds me of a friend who served two tours in Iraq as a Marine. In response to my question of why he joined the service, he recalled the story of going to a recruitment presentation in college where members of each of the major branches of service presented the opportunities and experiences available in their respective services. One by one, members of the Army, Navy, and Air Force stood in dress uniform and for ten minutes presented the advantages of their branch and all it had to offer. The last to speak was a gruff Marine sergeant who went to the podium and said two sentences: "We're not going to give you anything. If you want to be a Marine, you'll have to earn everything you get." Then he went back to his chair and sat down. My friend said that's when he decided to be a Marine.

This approach is the way Jesus encountered people who showed an interest in him and his ministry. He consistently set a high bar for entry with newcomers, often challenging them to the point that he drove them away. At one point he even told an assembled group of casual followers (who were looking to literally be fed) that to join him they must be willing to eat his flesh and drink his blood (John 6:53–66), which to them sounded like madness.

But once people were committed, Jesus went to extreme lengths to connect and serve them. He made the yoke of following him easy and the discipleship burden light, demonstrating immense patience, interest, and love—even after they denied him publicly and ran away in fear for their own lives.

Jesus' approach of high bar for entry and low bar for maintaining relationship allowed him to filter out those who were not truly committed to his mission to be disciples and disciple-makers. It created the right audience for him, giving him confidence that those who hung around would finish the task and be equipped and trained to lead the church.

A DMM approach is similar in concept. We share what God has done and is now doing, and explain the reality of the kingdom of God and his call on their life. Those who are interested and looking for God—and who God has already been drawing to himself—are eager to join in the process; it's an easy "sell." Those who aren't we continue to love and maintain relationship, but we don't invest much time with them. This allows us to focus our efforts on those who are ready to grow.

This approach may sound cultic, and if it were coupled with a "come" strategy (see *Contrast #2* on page 91) it could even result in a cultlike environment. But when coupled with a "go" strategy it assures that those who come into the organization are ones that will in fact take the message and the calling to others.

It sets up multiplication, because those in the network of relationships are all on the same page in terms of process and on board in terms of commitment level. It allows our communication to be focused and consistent. It allows for the next generation of disciples to be made efficiently, without having to invest time and energy in those who are only casually committed and involved.

Contrast #17 – Onboarding:
Visitor vs. Sponsored Connection

Onboarding is a common marketplace term describing the process of how people join an organization, such as the steps required for new employees to join a company, get acclimated, and begin their work. Ideally, companies want to make the process as effective and efficient as possible so they become productive quickly.

Churches also have an onboarding process that guides and directs newcomers as they engage in the church's activities and practice their faith in a way that aligns with the church's mission and vision. The effectiveness of this process is critical for how believers engage in disciple-making. If it is fuzzy or poorly executed, believers will not engage in making disciples, much less making disciples that make disciples.

Unknown and Disconnected Visitor

In a CAWKI setting, new people typically come into the church as visitors to the congregational service. They may be a total stranger, or may have been invited by a current attender. But even if they were invited, they are still relationally disconnected to the church as a whole and are "outsiders" to its life and culture.

The church's programming must hold the interest of this broad and varied group of people in order to retain them as weekly attenders. The church's success ultimately hinges on its ability to encourage newcomers to take the next step, an approach typically based on appealing to their interests (as discussed in *Contrast #16 – Invitation: Appeal vs. Call [page 152]*). This usually involves some kind of orientation where they can learn more and get connected to various serving opportunities or programs of interest. The ultimate outcome of onboarding for most churches is to have people officially join as members.

This broad-to-narrow onboarding process is often lengthy and unpredictable. It takes a long time for visitors to move to the point of full engagement. Even more challenging is that it sets the commitment bar very low at the beginning then attempts to raise it as the process continues (also discussed in see *Contrast #16* on page 152). It's nearly impossible to determine in advance what commitment level a visitor will eventually settle into.

Ultimately, only a minority will be fully committed to the church's mission and vision. This creates an awkward situation both for the church and the visitor/attender who knows he's not engaged. The church's programming must still accommodate him, but what's the nature of the relationship between him and the church?

I tend to believe this broad-to-narrow, low-to-high bar onboarding approach is well-intentioned. I also believe it is seen as an attempt to model Jesus' acceptance of anyone

> Jesus' approach of high-bar for entry and low-bar for maintaining relationship allowed him to filter out those who were not truly committed to his mission to be disciples and disciple-makers.

without regard to their previous church experience, faith stance, or beliefs. But it is time- and energy-consuming, awkward, unpredictable and inefficient. Unfortunately, because visitors are the lifeblood of the church the CAWKI model leaves few alternatives; this is the process the legacy church is married to if it wants to grow.

Connected and Called Disciple

In DMM, "newcomers" or "visitors" is an unusual concept. As an example, in our branch of DMM we don't publicize our gatherings or group/church leaders' contact information. The gatherings are not the focus in a DMM—relational discipleship is. There is no visitor stream to accommodate since believers in the church are "going" to meet and engage with others (rather than encouraging others to "come" to church). When they do, they encourage the people they've engaged with to start their own group with their own relational network.

It is rare for a visitor to show up to a network church gathering unannounced or unaware of what the gathering is all about. But even when new people do onboard they are typically sponsored (i.e., someone has invited them or has a previous relationship connection with them). Since the believers are usually discipling a limited number of people they have greater availability to spend time with the newcomers to get them onboarded personally and efficiently.

Since being a disciple and making disciples is the focus of all the interactions, it makes the onboarding process very focused. The calling to be a committed disciple is the high-bar front-end of the onboarding process. Those who aren't ready or motivated toward being a disciple self-select out of the process immediately. And because the process is simple it is easily reproduced. The way each new disciple is engaged is how they engage with the people they disciple.

All these components set up for multiplication to occur. The process removes all the unnecessary hurdles and hoops that block discipleship multiplication, and leaves in the most vital, important step: Surrendering one's life to Christ as King and Lord.

Contrast #18 – Converts' Cultural Impact: Extraction vs. Infusion

Over the last century or so we've learned this truth in international missions: It's much more effective for indigenous people to communicate the gospel to their own culture than it is for an outsider (e.g., a Westerner) to communicate a North American "version" of the gospel pre-loaded with its unique language and cultural characteristics. The vast cultural distance between the two groups introduces barriers to understanding and trust that must be interpreted and translated.

What's true in international missions at a macro-cultural level is equally true—although at a much smaller scale—for communicating the gospel within North America at a micro-cultural level. Even when we speak the same language (i.e., English), there are unique differences in every set of relationships in our society. This also includes differences between those who are churched and those who aren't. The legacy church has its own unique culture that is separate and distinct from the culture of the world it is called to reach.

The reality and impact of this "churched" cultural barrier may be difficult to discern if you've lived in it for very long. But it is real, even if it is subtle.

Extraction

When people come to participate in a legacy church programming they are leaving their "tribe" and culture. By tribe, I mean their family, friends, and other important connections with people they know. Their culture includes all facets of their relationships and way of life: Common experiences, history, language, customs, habits, traditions, mores, etc. They leave their current tribe and culture, come to a church culture to practice their faith then return to their original culture for the remainder of the week. This extracts them from the people with whom they have the greatest affinity, the highest credibility, and the deepest level of trust. Over time, as their engagement in the legacy model continues, their tribal relationship ties begin to atrophy as they adopt the language and culture of the church. They gradually appear as an outsider to their tribe. Sooner or later, these relationship ties with their tribe may be even severed altogether. To those remaining in the tribe, their former tribe member's departure can create confusion and resentment. Ultimately, the remaining tribe members may reject Jesus and the gospel, seeing them as outside influences that pulled one of their members away.

Infusion

In DMM, people are sharing their faith and practicing discipleship inside their current culture and with the members of their tribe. They are able to use the elements of their common culture to talk about Jesus; they leverage their common history and expressions to introduce the truth of the gospel and the call to follow Jesus. Those hearing the gospel are able to see genuine—and culturally meaningful—life transformation. The gospel is expressed in common terms and ways from someone they know and trust. There are no cultural biases or barriers to resolve or overcome.

This approach infuses disciples—each with their personal redemption stories—into the harvest of potential disciples-to-be. This legitimizes the call to follow Jesus is in a way that extraction simply can't achieve, because infusion eliminates all the cultural barriers. It brings a level of authenticity to the gospel for those who haven't yet heard it. There's nothing to cloud or confuse what it means to surrender your life, trust in Jesus, and follow his example of life and faith. It is the removal of barriers that allows for quick and efficient discipleship within the tribal networks.

The reality and impact of this "churched" cultural barrier may be difficult to discern if you've lived in it for very long. But it is real, even if it is subtle.

There are some who might say the gospel and its truth stands on its own and is relevant in any culture. I would agree with this. However, infusion is not about changing the gospel message, it's about communicating the gospel message effectively. With an infusion approach, the only barrier to overcome is the spiritual barrier of belief—which is as it should be. The gospel doesn't and shouldn't call for us to dispense with our culture and replace it with a church culture. Instead the gospel calls us to redeem culture. Infusion promotes this, and extraction simply can't.

Contrast #19 – Membership Requirements: Compliance vs. Obedience

What does "membership" mean? Technically, it is the state or status of belonging to a defined, organized group; or the group viewed as a whole. But what do you associate with the term as a modern-day Christian in the West?

Contrasting "membership" is challenging. While it is a well-defined concept in CAWKI, the designation doesn't really exist in a DMM. So for the sake of discussion I will assume that membership in a DMM implies someone who is actively participating and supporting the church's vision and mission, and representing its values well.

Exclusive Compliance

CAWKI, by and large, views membership from organizational, democratic, judicial, and perhaps even legal perspectives. This kind of membership is analogous to participation in many other social organizations, such as a local fitness club, neighborhood associations, Lions Club, etc.

CAWKI membership is exclusive. It describes a set of people with explicit privileges granted only to people on the list. As an example, even if someone is a member in good standing in their own church they still don't have the same standing in another church.

The most obvious component of church membership is the granting of voting rights in corporate decisions (depending on the church's polity) like fiscal issues and pastoral searches. Membership gives people a way to participate in certain (though typically limited) situations, giving the congregation what amounts to affirmation participation: They approve or reject initiatives proposed by the leadership of the church.

Often, membership status is attained through a class where requirements are presented and the commitment to comply is formalized and documented. The degree to which churches vet the membership applicants varies between congregations, or course, but often the process defaults to trusting the applicants on the information they provide. In some denominations, membership can be transferred between local congregations.

Membership expectations often center on compliance to church policies or membership codes, agreement with doctrinal statements, etc. Membership defines the minimum standard of behavior people must adhere to in order to qualify or maintain member status. It is hoped, of course, that members will do much more than the minimum. But from an organizational standpoint, CAWKI defines membership as mutual agreement to what amounts to a lowest common denominator of standards.

Inclusive Obedience

DMM has a relational view on membership. Meaning, your status is determined by your participation with other believers you're ministering with and the nature of the relationships you have with them and with God. The higher quality these relationships are the more influential you will be in the church.

Membership in a DMM ministry is inclusive. If you're a follower of Jesus you have full rights and privileges. You're a part of the universal church no matter where you happen to live on the planet. Paul, in particular, illustrates membership as being a vital part of a human body, where each part plays a role in the health and function of the body no matter how inconspicuous or undignified it may be.

Each DMM is free to operationally involve its members in the organization as it sees fit, which could involve a democratic process. In our particular branch, we give individual churches the autonomy to decide issues at the home-church level (how to distribute money, how to serve others, when and where to meet, how to handle conflict, how to onboard newcomers, etc.). However, we establish and model love and unity as the standard in group dynamics.

Membership in DMM is granted not by the organization, but by God himself. This follows the biblical pattern, as seen in Ephesians (in this case granting inclusion to Gentile believers):

- "Consequently, you are no longer foreigners and strangers, but fellow citizens with God's people and also members of his household, built on the foundation of the apostles and prophets, with Christ Jesus himself as the chief cornerstone. In him the whole building is joined together and rises to become a holy temple in the Lord. And in him you too are being built together to become a dwelling in which God lives by his Spirit" (Eph. 2:19–22).
- "In reading this, then, you will be able to understand my insight into the mystery of Christ ... This mystery is that through the gospel the Gentiles are heirs together with Israel, members together of one body, and sharers together in the promise in Christ Jesus" (Eph. 3:4–6).
- "You were taught, with regard to your former way of life, to put off your old self, which is being corrupted by its deceitful desires; to be made new in the attitude of your minds; and to put on the new self, created to be like God in true righteousness and holiness. Therefore each of you must put off falsehood and speak

truthfully to your neighbor, for we are all members of one body"
(Eph. 4:22–25).

Instead of identifying a minimum set of standards for members
to comply with, DMM sets the bar extremely high. The context for
membership is a follower of Jesus who surrenders all of their life to
him. Jesus is both the source and accountability of all spiritual authority. So being a member in good standing of a DMM means consistent
obedience— keeping and responding to Jesus' commands and the
leading of the Holy Spirit—and the practice of disciple-making principles. This, in essence, is Jesus' comments about the outcome of obedience to his commands. We will know obedience by the spiritual fruit it
produces (Matt. 7:15–20, Luke 6: 43–44) and by the wisdom it creates
in people's choices (Matt. 7:24–27, Luke 6:47–49).

In this way, establishing "membership requirements" is superflu-
ous—all believers should be aiming for the
same "prize of the upward call" (Phil. 3:14).
If someone doesn't practice Jesus' commands,
the result is an unfruitful spiritual life that
will be evident to anyone observing it. The
outcome of a lack of obedience is the loss of
credibility and fruitfulness in the kingdom.

> Establishing "membership requirements" is superfluous—all believers should be aiming for the same "prize of the upward call" (Phil. 3:14).

Discussing membership this way may appear critical (like many
of the other contrasts in Section 2), and perhaps minor and nit-picky.
I assure you this is not my intention. Rather, I submit to you that
church membership is one of the many items we inherited in the
form of church introduced into the West. As I discussed in chapter
3, a compliance attitude toward following Jesus is another hold-over
from the paradigm we inherited as far back as early Catholicism. My
point is that we simply haven't evaluated membership because it's part

and parcel of the overall model and there isn't a convenient, viable substitute to put in its place.

Membership as it's structured in the CAWKI model does not reflect the New Testament picture of being members together of the body of Christ. That's not to say it's worldly or evil, just different from what's presented in the New Testament church. As such it's just another unnecessary element that gets in the way of multiplication.

Contrast #20 – Maturity Mindset: Externally Fed vs. Self-Fed

The focus of this contrast is directly related to the topic of self-perception discussed in see *Contrast #5* on page 101. The different identities (adherent vs. disciple-maker) also bring much different mindsets on how we go about growing in faith maturity. Each identity favors its own approach to things like how we get direction, insight and self-awareness, how we acquire knowledge of spiritual truth, and, ultimately, how we become more like Jesus.

Dependent and Passive
A legacy ministry approach reinforces a perception that spiritual maturity comes through learning and participation in church programming (as discussed in *Contrast #7 – Primary Method: Teaching vs. Training* [page 108], and *Contrast #13 – Maturity Gauge: Knowledge vs. Christlikeness* [page 136]). Truth comes through a limited number of "authorized and equipped" teachers, whether this is one of the church's programmed elements like the weekly sermon or an external resource like listening to an online message from a favorite Bible teacher. It all maintains a subtle atmosphere that keeps the laity dependent and passive, feeding a mindset that people should not and cannot depend

upon themselves and the Holy Spirit to guide them into all truth (see John 16:13–15).

Consider the combined, cumulative impact from some of the contrasts raised previously:

- A "location" organizational identity (see *Contrast #1* on page 88)
- A "come" orientation to the world (see *Contrast #2* on page 91)
- A hierarchical organizational structure (see *Contrast #4* on page 97)
- A personal identity as adherents (see *Contrast #5* on page 101)
- A primary methodology of teaching (see *Contrast #6* on page 106)
- A programmatic ministry application (see *Contrast #10* on page 119)
- A congregational primary meeting structure (see *Contrast #11* on page 123)
- A clergy leadership model (see *Contrast #12* on page 128)
- Using knowledge as the gauge for maturity (see *Contrast #13* on page 136)
- Emphasizing the gifts of teaching and pastoring, while de-emphasizing the gifts of apostleship and prophecy (see *Contrast #14* on page 139)
- A controlling management approach (see *Contrast #15* on page 146)
- An appeal-based invitation (see *Contrast #16* on page 152)
- Extracting people from their personal network and culture (see *Contrast #18* on page 158)
- A compliance-orientation to community membership (see *Contrast #19* on page 161)

Taken as a whole, it's obvious why people brought up in this environment look to the church to take the primary role in equipping them for maturity.

As an example, consider the common phrase often proudly uttered even by mature believers seeking for a church to join: "I'm looking for a church where I can be fed." This statement has been elevated in many instances to the point where it's missionized. That is to say, churches see "feeding" (usually interpreted as extensive exegetical teaching) as its missional responsibility. In response, individual Christians adopt the mindset of "being fed" as their own missional responsibility—even though they already have extremely high levels of Bible knowledge.

Interdependent and Active
A disciple-multiplying movement encourages and motivates believers to become self-feeding in regard to maturing in their faith. Each believer is expected to take ownership of their development and take the initiative when it comes to things like knowledge of God's word, spiritual discipline, hearing from the Holy Spirit, spiritual direction, spiritual warfare, strength to endure and prosper in times of hardship, persecution, or suffering, etc. This mindset creates a higher level of confidence and active engagement for putting discipleship principles into practice.

This mindset agrees with the biblical perspective that believers are more than equipped to "feed" themselves spiritually. Perhaps the clearest example of this is from 2 Peter:

"His divine power has given us everything we need for a godly life through our knowledge of him who called us by his own glory and goodness. Through these he has given us his very great and precious promises, so that through them you may participate in the divine nature, having escaped the corruption in the world caused by evil desires." (2 Pet. 1:3–4)

There are a number of things we emphasize in our branch of DMM regarding the typical and expected ways individual disciple-makers are to feed themselves:

- Read the Bible daily (see Ps. 119:9–16)
- Consistent and abiding prayer (see Phil. 4:6–7; Eph. 6:18)
- Resist the enemy (see Matt. 4:1–10; 1 Pet. 5:6–11)
- Prepare for persecution (see 2 Tim. 3:12–13)

When people are this focused on prayer and reading Scripture, in a posture of complete dependency on the Holy Spirit—who's role it is to convict us of sin and righteousness and to reveal spiritual truth to our unspiritual minds—growth toward spiritual maturity is a natural outcome.

Of course, believers are encouraged to seek out other spiritual life resources as a complement to their own personal self-feeding. We have the luxury of living at a time where these resources are vast and readily accessible. But these resources are always seen as a second, complementary step to self-feeding and not the first step that may create dependency upon them.

> Churches see "feeding" (usually interpreted as extensive exegetical teaching) as its missional responsibility. In response, individual Christians adopt the mindset of "being fed" as their own missional responsibility—even though they already have extremely high levels of Bible knowledge.

The idea of self-feeding is often a sticking point in discussing DMM's viability to those in the legacy church. Some argue that people who haven't been properly instructed are in no position to lead others to spiritual maturity; that the resulting outcome is effectively the blind leading the blind.

While the point is a valid technical concern, it is usually not a practical one. First, new disciples have personal faith mentors walking with them to correct and train as necessary and keep them heading in the right direction.

Secondly, additional training resources can easily be leveraged as needed to provide truth or answer questions or concerns that come up.

We want believers to have the mindset of being both responsible for their own spiritual maturity and capable of attaining it (under the guidance and leadership of the Holy Spirit). When this mindset is passed on to new generations of disciples it contributes to movements that are spiritually hungry, eager to learn and be transformed, and even more eager to obey.

9 How People Engage with the Church

The task of leadership is not to put greatness into humanity,
but to elicit it, for the greatness is there already.

—John Buchan

The previous chapter looked at how the organization of church engaged with individuals. Now we flip that interaction around to view how individuals engage with the organization of church. This chapter looks at how individuals view and participate in the ministry of the church.

```
┌─ Church Engagement Contrasts ──────────────────┐
│ 21 – Participation:                             │
│           Passive Attendance vs. Active Obedience│
│ 22 – Interaction:                               │
│           Knowledge Sharing vs. Mutual Accountability│
│ 23 – New Believer Engagement:                   │
│           Delayed vs. Immediate                 │
│ 24 – Faith Errors:                              │
│           Hidden vs. Exposed                    │
│ 25 – Faith Model:                               │
│           The Sr. Pastor vs. Your Discipler     │
└─────────────────────────────────────────────────┘
```

Contrast #21 – Participation:
Passive Attendance vs. Active Obedience

One of the general truths of human behavior is that what we do is driven by what we believe. Said another way: Our actions will usually align with what we believe to be true. There's also a corollary: We tend to avoid actions that conflict with our beliefs.

Applying this truth in a church context provides some insight into the legacy church model and how people participate in it. How the church operates ultimately is a reflection of our belief about the church's purpose. This reflects equally on both the church as an organization and on the individuals who participate in it.

Passive Attendance

The primary way people participate in a legacy church is by attending a worship gathering, as discussed in *Contrast #11 – Primary Meeting Structure: Congregation vs. Small Group* (page 123). This gathering is a one-on-many event, where one person (or at times more than one) ministers to many. With the exception of those who volunteer in a service role to support a program like children's ministry, hospitality, worship, etc., the vast majority of people participating in church are observing others take active roles.

Consider the example of the average congregational service in the legacy church. The programming for the service has been pre-determined, often many weeks in advance. The overall theme for the service is determined by the church staff and is then communicated to the congregation. Often the worship focus is pre-framed for the congregation by the worship leader who might, for example, highlight a song's content or give a personal testimony about why the song is meaningful. The important elements of the sermon are conveyed to the congregation by the person preaching based upon personal and individual study. Suggestions on how to apply the truths in the passages are also provided.

Taken as a whole, the experience of church attenders is passive. Someone else is studying, thinking, praying, searching, and revealing insight. There's little opportunity for those in the audience to personally discover, to hear directly from God in a way that hasn't been filtered through others—however qualified or relevant they may be.

The subtle danger in setting up a passive experience in church is it creates an expectation that attenders don't (or perhaps can't, or shouldn't?) hear from God reliably. If we always do people's studying, thinking, praying, searching, wrestling with God or defining how to apply the Bible for them, how will they do it for themselves?

Why would they?

Beyond the congregational gathering, attenders increasing their participation means attending additional activities or events such as a Sunday School or mid-size group, small group, men's/women's ministry gathering, or some other specialty-focused events (membership, discipleship, leadership class, etc.). Many of these opportunities are teaching-oriented events also using a one-on-many approach (e.g., knowledge is passed on to participants by a Bible study leader).

Of course, there are many in the legacy church who spend significant amounts of time dedicated to personal devotions, study, and serving others, both in the church and out in the community. Likewise, there are many legacy churches that sponsor and encourage active participation beyond the congregational gathering. These are obvious and commendable.

My point is not to insinuate that active participation never occurs in the legacy church, or that CAWKI somehow fails to encourage participants to actively practice their faith. However, I am highlighting that active participation is not the primary experience of many who attend the legacy church. Instead, the most basic and universal means of participation are passive.

Active Obedience

As highlighted in *Contrast #19 – Membership Requirements: Compliance vs. Obedience* (page 161), obedience is one of the key factors in producing discipleship multiplication. In contrast #19 the focus was membership requirements; here it is participation in the church's mission.

> If we always do people's studying, thinking, praying, searching, wrestling with God or defining how to apply the Bible for them, how will they do it for themselves? Why would they?

It could be argued that obedience is the most basic application of following Jesus in faith. It's so simple even a child can do it—and unless our faithful response to God mimics that childlike simplicity we've missed the point of faith altogether. Obedience is the first step toward following Jesus, taken even before the willful decision to trust in Jesus' atoning work on the cross. Trust-centered obedience is the foundation every other faith practice is built upon, and it is the single-greatest indicator of faith maturity.

For some, "obedience" may imply a legalistic, cultic, or authoritative obligation to human leadership—which is absolutely not the way to see it. Obedience in disciple-making refers to Jesus' call in Matthew 28:19 to teach others to obey his commands. As noted in *Definitions*, the Greek word for "obey" (*tereo*) used here means *to watch over, guard, keep,* or *observe.* In the context of disciple-making and being a disciple it means to live as Jesus lived, adopting his priorities and deliberately and consistently practicing his teachings and way of life.

It also means to model his practical dependence upon the Father and his willingness to respond to the promptings and leadings of the Holy Spirit. In our DMM branch, we refer to it as IRCO: Immediate,

Radical, Costly Obedience. It includes the willingness to do what might appear illogical in response to God's leading, with zero lag time between hearing God and our response. Think of all the great heroes of the faith in the Bible: The greatest examples all demonstrated an obedience that was immediate, total, often radical or illogical in its context, and even costly—sometimes at the threat of loss of life.

This kind of obedience simply cannot be built through passive approaches. Watching other people's obedience can certainly be encouraging and motivational, but each disciple must practice obedience on their own. They must learn to hear the Good Shepherd's unfiltered, unmodified and unqualified "voice." They must trust the Holy Spirit's promptings and leadings which are given in the moment and specifically intended for them.

Learning and building the discipline of obedience takes practice over time, and there simply are no shortcuts. Obedience (like discipleship as a whole) is not something you know; it's something you do. Learning about obedience is a great first step, but if it's not practiced it adds next to nothing to deepening your faith. Jesus himself obeyed the Father as an aspect of knowing him, so it should be no surprise that we must also.[1]

It may be helpful to think of it this way: The opposite of obedience is not disobedience. The opposite of obedience is self-will. We can have churches full of people who act like Christians (whatever that means) and do Christian things, but who are passively failing to hear and respond to God. When we fail to hear and obey God, by default we go our own way—the way that seems best to us.

Following Jesus in obedience is not a formula or a static religion. Instead, following Jesus is a relationship with the living God who is actively working in and among his people for purposes beyond their personal self-improvement and enrichment. Obedience ultimately is the acknowledgement of surrendering our lives to Jesus in response to all he has done. It is offering ourselves as living sacrifices (Rom. 12:–2), not an offering to gain mercy from God but offering in response to mercy he's already given. The proper response is to live our entire lives as if they are on the altar as an act of worship to Him—which allows us to discern His will. Anything less than complete surrender simply doesn't make any sense: "Why do you call me 'Lord, Lord,' and not do what I say?" (Luke 6:46).

Obedience is practiced by everyone in DMM at virtually every level. Non-believers learn from the very first conversations that God is trustworthy and will lead them to the truth. They are taught and expected to actively look for God to reveal himself and his truth from the Bible, and to trust and follow his leading. Believers are expected and encouraged to listen to and follow the Holy Spirit as a foundation for faith practice.

> The opposite of obedience is not disobedience. The opposite of obedience is self-will. We can have churches full of people who act like Christians (whatever that means) and do Christian things, but who are passively failing to hear and respond to God.

Obedience begins with daily Bible reading where the emphasis is hearing from God not just to know the content but to put it into practice so we can be transformed. It comes in prayer where listening to God is as important as reciting our requests to him; we listen with intent to hear and obey. It comes in knowing who to talk to about Jesus and discerning who is ready to respond to God (often it's not the people naturally we think). It comes in conversation with others when the Holy Spirit leads us on what to say and not say, as we become aware of what others are dealing with below the surface.

176

It comes at the group level where we create a weekly cadence of mutual accountability around practicing what we collectively heard from God.

From a church model standpoint, this discussion comes down to one of two possibilities:

1. The church believes its mission is best accomplished by its members being passive participants, or
2. The church believes its mission is best accomplished by its members being active participants.

If we believe our mission is to produce passive participants then we can continue to do what we've been doing for centuries. But if we believe our mission is for believers to be active in spreading the gospel, being responsive in the moment to the leading of the Holy Spirit, and participating in making disciples of all nations, wouldn't we be more focused on equipping and training each believer to take an active role?

Contrast #22 – Interaction: Knowledge Sharing vs. Mutual Accountability

What does it look like when Christians gather together? What kind of interaction do they have?

What does a typical gathering include? What should it include?

These are discovery questions, not accusative ones. Meaning, how often have we thought about what we should do when we gather? In my informal surveys, the answers I most often get are not surprising. They include worship, fellowship, looking into God's word, and to a lesser extent things like service and helping those in need. All great answers, and perfectly appropriate to the body of Christ.

There's one answer I almost never get, however; and it's what this contrast addresses. I'm calling it accountability. This is often a heavy word, with connotations of legalistic, works-oriented, "don't-mess-up" oversight; like we're all waiting for you to fail. Nothing could be further from the truth.

Occasionally someone will respond to the survey with "spur one another on to love and good deeds," which is close. Accountability means being clear on what you intend to do and then taking responsibility to complete it. In the context of a group this effort becomes mutual, meaning that everyone participates in taking ownership and supporting each other to accomplish what's in our hearts. It is an entirely positive and supportive, community activity.

Knowledge-Centered Interaction
One of the standard approaches in a legacy setting for people who wish to go deeper in their faith is to join a Bible study. Because the goal of a Bible study is to study the Bible, the primary activity involves participants exchanging Bible knowledge and facilitating mutual learning. This is a wonderful goal and can be a great part of the experience of Christian community. But it is limited when it comes to making disciples that can and will make more disciples.

I've previously discussed many of the implications of CAWKI's emphasis on teaching (see *Contrast #14* on page 139) and its use of knowledge as a gauge of maturity (see *Contrast #13* on page 136). To summarize here, a natural outcome of the legacy approach is that knowledge sharing becomes the goal of their fellowship. There may/ may not be a focus on applying the knowledge or discussing how it's transforming individuals' lives.

Of course, this is not to suggest that all Bible studies in legacy churches are focused on simply exchanging information. Nor is it to suggest that believers in legacy churches don't pursue application of the passages they study. I've personally been a part of some group studies where deep and lasting friendships were forged, where people experienced significant life transformation.

Yet even with these results and the fellowship that came with it, I was not inspired or challenged to apply my new knowledge and growth into a disciple-making emphasis. The gains were predominantly focused on my personal sanctification. I suspect the same is true for a great number of believers participating in legacy church Bible studies.

Obedience-Centered Interaction
When people gather together in a DMM, the interaction is based on obedience, not just learning.

There's a difference between …

A. Reading the Scriptures in order to learn the content, and
B. Reading the Scriptures for the purpose of hearing God with the intent to obey what he reveals.

The latter involves a much more open-hearted, surrendered posture. It involves listening with expectation. It involves a spirit of obedience and faithful trust.

It also involves a level of group accountability that the average Bible study probably doesn't have. As mentioned in *Contrast #11 – Primary Meeting Structure: Congregation vs. Small Group* [page 123], the primary DMM gathering is a small group (our branch calls them ⅓rds groups). Each weekly group meeting involves a "look back" time to recount how everyone obeyed what

Accountability means being clear on what you intend to do and then taking responsibility to complete it. In the context of a group this effort becomes mutual, meaning that everyone participates in taking ownership and supporting each other to accomplish what's in our hearts.

God revealed to them in the previous meeting, as well as "look up" time where group members read and discuss Bible passages to receive insight and revelation from God.

The last segment is the "look forward" time where group members discuss how they plan to obey.

Participants share with each other:

1. What they believe/understand God to be revealing to them in the Bible passage,
2. God's personal message on how they can and should respond in obedience,
3. Who they will share this passage with, and
4. How they can use the truths in the passage to train someone else.

The result is the entire group becomes invested in each other's points of obedience, which could include praying for or supporting each other and even helping out by participating with them. These points are written down in a journal and reviewed at the next meeting to discuss the outcome.

The regular rhythm of mutual accountability this creates is both encouraging and effective. It's a potent reminder that our faith is rarely an individual exercise, that we are connected to each other as we grow to be like Jesus. And it encourages believers to apply what they learn toward immediate application in discipling someone else.

In addition to the group-level accountability, we also emphasize a deeper, more personal level of accountability. This typically involves two or three people of the same gender who meet regularly (ideally weekly) to discuss (primarily) two things:

1. What God is revealing to them in their personal reading of Scripture, and, in response, what they should start or stop doing, correct, or how they can grow, and

2. How they are doing at avoiding sin and resisting the influence of the world.

The first point is built around 1 Timothy 3:16–17: That the word of God is inspired by him and useful for everything Jesus' followers need to continue growing in Christlikeness. The second point is based upon 1 John 2:15–17: That believers should avoid identifying with or pursuing things of the world and all its influences that include lust of the eyes and flesh as well as the pride of life. These relationships allow for accountability around items that may not be appropriate in mixed-gender or larger groups.

Practicing both levels of accountability together ensures people are putting into practice what they are hearing from God. It ensures a level of purity with a practical and appropriate level of confidentiality. It creates a mutuality in the church as we encourage, support, and "spur one another on" to live like Jesus.

Contrast #23 – New Believer Engagement: Delayed vs. Immediate

The training process for producing airplane pilots has a counter-intuitive step: Pilot trainees complete their first solo long before they are fully skilled or licensed to fly. In fact, it's normal to only have between ten to twenty hours of flying experience before they are required to fly in the pilot seat, alone. In essence, pilot trainees are taught just enough to keep them from crashing before flying solo for the first time. But flying alone is a key step in learning to fly well.

The principle behind training pilots is equally applicable for training disciples. Discipling early is a key developmental step in learning to disciple. Plus, if we try to teach a new disciple everything they need

181

to know before asking them to disciple another person it's very likely they won't ever do so.

Delay In Order to Teach

As mentioned in *Contrast #7 – Primary Method: Teaching vs. Training* [page 108], the legacy church typically defines discipling as mentoring and teaching someone who's already a professed believer, helping them to become more knowledgeable in the Scriptures, to understand the key doctrines and to reach a high level of maturity in their faith. This definition drives a heartfelt conviction that it's not appropriate for new Christians to engage in discipling others until they are mature or equipped. This approach carries several key implications that must be considered.

To start with, this approach takes a long time to produce a disciple. Because this process is so knowledge-centered it requires lots of preparation. It takes time to train people to a sufficiently high standard that they could be considered adequate "teachers" who are qualified to instruct others.

This also limits the number of disciple-makers. Many of the qualified "teaching disciple-makers" are likely already involved in other roles in the church, such as preaching or leading another programmed group.

The approach also limits the number of disciples that can be made. The avenues and opportunities for being discipled simply don't exist. Many churches try to get around this by offering separate discipleship programming. But the additional programming is often impractical because it requires participants to invest additional time over and above what they're currently committed to.

The entire process is elongated and inefficient. It does not produce many disciples, nor does it allow for multiplication to occur.

Release In Order to Train

In contrast to the legacy perspective, discipling in a DMM starts much sooner—in fact, immediately. Discipling starts from the very first conversation with people who are seeking God. They learn about a God who answers prayer and who can and often does things only God could do to prove his existence and his love for them. They learn that he intervenes in their lives uniquely and personally revealing himself to each individual. Seekers are encouraged and expected to begin practicing obedience to Christ and sharing their experiences with others they know. These are indicators of faithfulness.

Having disciple-making conversations early is both practical and advisable because new believers aren't asked to be teachers. They are asked simply to pass on what they know, even if it's one truth they learned from the Bible or one answered prayer. Their story or answered prayer or one simple truth is valid in the eyes of those they would share with.

We see this early (in many cases pre-conversion) obedience and discipleship in a number of places in the New Testament. Andrew had spent one afternoon with Jesus before inviting his brother Peter, saying "We have found the Messiah" (John 1.41–42). Philip, fresh off his introduction to Jesus, invites Nathanael to come and see "the one who Moses wrote about" (John 1:43–46). The Samaritan woman that Jesus encountered at Jacob's well went back to the town (as an outcast, by the way) and told the entire town, who ended up believing in Jesus (John 4:39–42). The man born blind and healed by Jesus defended Jesus to the Sanhedrin prior to his own belief (John 9:13–38). Apollos had been speaking influentially about Jesus even though he'd known only the baptism of John before Priscilla and Aquilla "explained the way of God more adequately" (Acts 18:24–26).

Early disciple-making activities like these train newcomers to the faith to be bold in their witness. As they come to faith and continue to grow, it supports their calling as disciple-makers. In effect, the sooner they start, the faster they become competent disciple-makers. And the most critical factor is the rate of discipleship multiplication increases, meaning more people come into the kingdom.

Contrast #24 – Faith Errors: Hidden vs. Exposed

One of the hallmarks of Christianity in the West has been a concern about upholding truth. The church as "the pillar and foundation of the truth" (1 Tim. 3:15) appropriately sees its role as stewarding the characterization of God and the accuracy of the Scriptures. It is natural that considering a different model of church would raise concerns about how truth is disseminated, practiced, encouraged, and upheld.

The Current Way
Faith errors (such as heresy, lack of knowledge and understanding, poor biblical interpretation, poor life choices, sinful habits, etc.) in a legacy ministry are often hidden. With so much of the programming being one-on-many formats and with so much of the activity being passive in nature, it's understandable that incorrect beliefs, values, or practices remain invisible for extended periods of time. There are fewer opportunities for these errors to surface.

The nature of the programming forces us to assume that those in the congregation agree with and adopt the content of a sermon. There are precious few feedback mechanisms to confirm learning or to interact with questions or even dissenting views.

184

The level of personal interaction and accountability for life choices can remain obscure or private. It's much easier for someone to attend church and remain on the sidelines as a practicing believer. Sometimes this is intentional, but often it is unintentional; the way the programming is set up simply doesn't allow for revealing what people are really thinking and how they are actually practicing their faith outside the church.

The New-Original Way
Faith errors in a disciple-making ministry are usually quickly exposed. The level and frequency of interaction provides very little space for things to remain hidden. Nearly everyone has a personal connection with someone who is actively discipling them, which accelerates the process of discovering and dealing with faith errors.

Let's be fair with this: CAWKI doesn't encourage faith errors. Nor does DMM guarantee absolute doctrinal and practical purity. If it did, most of the New Testament epistles would have been unnecessary since so many of them were written to deal with specific issues of faith errors. Dealing with faith errors will be an issue for the church until Jesus returns.

That said, the concern by those with a legacy church background over the ability of a DMM to uphold the truth is a persistent theme. Usually it's based on the presumption that the lack of qualified pastors and teachers in every gathering means there's no way to maintain truth. But this presumption is misleading on several levels.

First, what most legacy church participants miss is the level of personal interaction and accountability that exists in a DMM. It is highly relational, and involves consistent and regular interaction with your discipling mentor. There is very little room to keep things secret or hidden. Things like beliefs, values, understanding, and practices are quickly revealed.

People in a DMM are responding to the call to be a disciple and a disciple-maker. If the discipling mentors have done their job, the casually committed or those looking for a new hip way to do church have already been filtered out. Those being discipled are in the process of surrendering their lives, realizing God is the answer to their lostness and they are motivated to change.

Finally, it's easy to dismiss the role of the Holy Spirit and the inspiration of God's word. The Spirit teaches, convicts, reveals, instructs, intercedes—all for the purpose of correcting. The Bible is "God-breathed, and useful for teaching, correcting, rebuking and training in righteousness" (2 Tim. 3:16). Consider that participants are encouraged to devote significant time to pray and read the Word daily—often measured in hours of prayer and number of chapters each day—to listen for God's instruction, to put it into practice, and then interact with each other about it all in an environment of high-accountability relationships.

I believe there is a pattern of over-dependence on our systems and approach in the Western church, at the expense of absolute dependence on the Holy Spirit to guide and direct a process only he can.

Have we lost trust in the ability of the Holy Spirit and the Bible to do its work?

I ask this not as an accusation; it is actually a confession—because that's exactly what I did. I've personally experienced God's rebuke surrounding my own trust in programming and the mechanisms of teaching I'd depended on in my fifteen years of vocational pastoral ministry. Of course I believed the Holy Spirit and the Bible played a role, and I gave them credit for the ministry fruit that resulted. But in my core, I still put my trust primarily on the human process. I've repented from this, yet still find it so easy to lean on my own understanding. My flesh consistently wants to depend on the model, the recipe—and even DMM can be a recipe if we allow it to be.

I'm not projecting this onto everyone, but I've talked to enough DMM practitioners coming out of a legacy model to know it is a regular theme. Experience tells me many—if not most—people who transition from CAWKI to DMM will encounter this at some point: I believe there is a pattern of over-dependence on our systems and approach in the Western church, at the expense of absolute dependence on the Holy Spirit to guide and direct a process as only he can.

Contrast #25 – Faith Model:
The Sr. Pastor vs. Your Discipler

Believers should ultimately look to Jesus Christ as the example on how to live and practice faith. That is obvious, and hopefully no matter what model of church organization we're using, we're all working toward imitating him in everything we do.

In addition to Jesus, it's important to have a present-day faith model; someone to look to for example and encouragement. This is well-established in the New Testament as a means of passing faith from one generation of disciples to the next. For example, Paul encourages the believers in Thessalonica,

"You know how we lived among you for your sake. You became imitators of us and of the Lord, for you welcomed the message in the midst of severe suffering with the joy given by the Holy Spirit. And so you became a model to all the believers in Macedonia and Achaia. The Lord's message rang out from you not only in Macedonia and Achaia—your faith in God has become known everywhere."(1 Thess. 1:5–8)

Modeling is, in part, a leadership practice (as discussed in see *Contrast #12* on page 128). It is influencing others toward an as-yet unachieved goal, paving the way for others to walk. How leaders practice faith sets the tone for the church.

The "Ideal" Model

The most visible person modeling faith in a legacy church ministry is typically the primary teaching pastor or senior minister in the church. Though in some churches there are multiple people in these roles, in most churches this is one and the same person. For the sake of simplicity, in this contrast I'll define this as the "senior minister."

At first glance, having the senior minister as the faith model might seem like a good idea; a no-brainer, in fact. But as counter-intuitive as this may sound, this approach can easily build unwanted barriers to making disciples.

If the person at the top of the hierarchical leadership structure is the faith model, then by default this is an unrealistic model to follow— unless, of course, the church expects every person in the congregation to become a senior minister.

In most churches, relational access to this person is limited. Real-world, life-on-life influence is virtually impossible to obtain. In small churches it's easier for senior ministers to know the parishioners, but they're still unable to invest significant time with each person. In larger churches senior ministers might know the parishioners at a basic level (name, occupation, etc.); and the larger the church the more prevalent this is. In very large churches, participants will never interact with the senior minister. This results in a kind of pseudo-celebrity relationship between the "model" of faith and those who are "following" the model.

The senior minister only has thirty to forty-five minutes a week to model behaviors, or convey truths, concepts, or convictions—and it's a one-way process at that. There's no way senior ministers can drill down to individual application with everyone who's in the congregation or watching online. At best they can provide general, high-level application and hope it's relevant to as many people under the bell curve as possible.

Having a single faith model limits the potential influence. No one person can be an effective model for everyone, which means there will be a relational distance between the senior minister and segments of the congregation. For instance, there could be feelings of inferiority due to the senior minister being an "ideal" believer. Or perhaps there's a lack of respect because the senior minister is younger, or from a different geographic region or ethnic background, or there's slightly different social views, etc. Congregants experiencing this distance simply don't relationally connect with the model, so trust isn't established and it lessens the potential for influence.

Churches will often look for a senior minister that fits a profile: someone who can relate to the church's target audience. By default, this approach segments the body; now part of the church is favored and part is not.

All these barriers reduce the modeling influence of the senior minister. Obviously senior ministers are not the only one modeling faith in the legacy church model. But the legacy church approach is set up so that all those who are looking for a faith model are looking toward the senior minister as the "ideal" model to follow.

The "Real" Model

The most visible person modeling faith in a disciple-multiplying movement is the mentor disciple (and by extension the person who disciples him/her). This is particularly true in the early stages of a new disciple's mentoring when the foundations of faith are set.

Mentor disciples have great opportunity for influence. They are readily accessible and interact with their disciples on a regular basis. New disciples' faith is shaped and grown through observation, through practice and through one-on-one conversations to clarify misunderstandings and further deepen perspective.

There's a vitally important context regarding discipleship mentoring to keep in mind. The discipleship mentor role isn't authoritarian or directive; it is a serving role. It is not set up as a human process of "I say, you do." Mentors act as guides to help new disciples achieve success and effectiveness in what they are called to do. The mentor models a faith practice, but God then directs specific steps of obedience to the disciple. The mentor then guides and steers toward deeper understanding and maturity through experience and wisdom.

> Modeling is where the discipleship rubber meets the road ... What new disciples see, experience, and practice is what gets passed down to the next generation of disciples; what isn't seen, experienced, or practiced does not.

This is a vastly different form of modeling than we see in most legacy church approaches where the teacher/trainer is positioned as the authority and the primary focus is on learning. New visitors coming into a legacy church setting will not have a personal guide to walk with them, and so they are left to their own initiative to get connected and find a discipleship mentor.

It is perhaps fitting to close this section of contrasts between CAWKI and DMM on this topic of modeling. Modeling is where the discipleship rubber meets the road: Virtually all the topics we've discussed here are evident in the experience of a disciple-maker modeling to a disciple. What new disciples see, experience, and practice is what gets passed down to the next generation of disciples; what isn't seen, experienced, or practiced does not.

It is only through discipling someone in such a way that they can disciple someone else that we truly grasp all that Jesus intended in the Great Commission. It's sobering but true: Without effective modeling, multiplication simply can't occur and we fail in our stewardship of Jesus' commands.

As we close this section and turn toward Part 3: The Way Forward, I encourage you: If you've never practiced DMM principles and practices before, begin now by modeling disciple-making to one individual who will obey and train others—just one! It is the most important and effective thing you can do to contribute to accomplishing God's purpose in our time.

Part 3:
The Way Forward

A review of specific strategies for deploying DMM,
as well as the implications they bring and
the impact of the changes the church will experience

10 Decision Points

One cool judgment is worth a dozen hasty councils. The thing to do is to supply light and not heat.

—William Shakespeare

After working through the 25 contrasts in part 2 you may have more questions than answers. You may feel a course correction is called for, but have no idea which direction to turn. You may feel this whole discussion is a big waste of time. Or you may feel that—*finally*—you have some language to put to the frustrations you've been experiencing. You may have picked up this book looking for strategy options in response to the COVID-19 pandemic.

Whatever you may be dealing with, I suggest one way forward: Stop, fast, and pray, and then respond (and the order is significant).

Stop

The absolute *worst* thing to do would be to roll out some half-baked, quick-fried, flavor-of-the-month, knee-jerk, Band-Aid disciple-making program. It'd be better to do nothing than to go with something that amounts to a reactionary recipe or a faddish add-on to your church's programming. Devote some time to reflection and to gain awareness of what impulses you're subjected to. Clear the decks of your mind to give you the time and space you need.

To help you stop I suggest an exercise of reflection. First, review each of the contrasts between disciple-multiplying movement and legacy ministry approaches listed in part 2. Next, choose the five that stand out the most to you, for whatever reason (which you may or may not be able to explain). It's fine if you have six or eight, but have a limited set to consider. Finally, consider the following questions:

- How does each impact the multiplication of disciple-makers, positively or negatively?
- For each contrast, what are the implications for ...
  - Individual believers?
  - Your congregation?
  - Other congregations across North America or the West?
  - The universal church?
- What are the implications for you as a leader or pastor in Jesus' church?
  - How does it impact your vision and/or expectations about yourself as a church leader?
  - What does it say about your role and the way you currently do ministry?
  - What does it expose that you didn't see previously?

Fast and Pray

Adopting a disciple-multiplying movement approach should, in my view, be preceded by prayer and fasting. Enter a season of fasting, so you'll be in a posture of dependence upon God and not relying on yourself or your own ministry experience. Pray as if your ministry depended completely on the Lord's guidance and provision—because it does!

You'll need to hear directly from the Lord, because this will likely feel like a reorientation. Moving from a legacy church approach to a disciple-multiplying movement approach means you'll probably be off the edge of almost every ministry map you've ever used.

As you position your heart and mind to hear from the Lord, listen for his guidance and direction. Moving forward into a DMM ministry will be counter-intuitive in so many ways. You'll want to be confident the Lord is leading you, instead of your history, experience, logic, etc.; resist the urge to create quick plans based on your own ability and instead let the Holy Spirit inform you first. Use the Scriptures as a guide. There's no advantage in rushing this; an effective DMM ministry needs to go slow anyway.

Assess your level of comfort and satisfaction with the kingdom return on the investments of time, energy, and finances you've poured into your legacy church ministry. Don't worry at this point about potential changes and the implications they bring (that's coming in the next chapters).

You particularly want to be aware of fear-driven thoughts. For instance, if you're a vocational minister you'll likely have career-related concerns that surface: What does it mean for my financial security, or my reputation? What will happen to the congregation? Those are valid and relevant concerns, but as significant as they seem they're actually secondary.

The point is to hear God's leading, and he does not lead us through fear: "There is no fear in love. But perfect love drives out fear … The one who fears is not made perfect in love" (1 John 4:18). So if God isn't the source of fear, who do you think is? Whatever happens will be steps of faith, and if the Lord leads the process he will work out the circumstances. Be aware of the fears, capture them and set them aside.

Respond

Now you are in position to respond to the Lord's leading. It's really simple at this point.

If the result of your reflection is an honest sense of contentment and a clear conscience, then my recommendation is to not implement any changes in your ministry. You can put this book away and continue doing what you've been doing.

If, however, you are discontent at any level you have a choice to make. You must confirm in your heart, mind and soul whether God is calling you to make a change. Then you must decide whether or not you will respond to that calling.

Moving into the unknown of DMM will not be based on convenience. It will likely contradict many of your ministry best practices, habits, and assumptions. Ask the Lord to give you courage and wisdom for the next steps in DMM (realizing they are still yet undefined). By design, this is a step of faith. When God called Abraham to leave his homeland in Ur of the Chaldeans, he didn't provide a GPS location on Abraham's smartphone with turn-by-turn navigation steps. He told Abraham to go "to the land which I *will* show you" (Gen. 12:1, emphasis mine). Don't be alarmed that you don't know every step of the way or have all the answers.

You'll want to eventually seek the counsel of others in a setting where you can explore and discuss options, implications and desired outcomes. This requires some wisdom, because there will be environments and groups where these conversations will not be constructive. Unfortunately, there may be precious few contemporaries or peers in your network with prior experience to lean on for opinion and perspective. Thankfully, the number of people discussing DMM as a viable ministry strategy has vastly increased in recent years. It won't be too hard to find people to interact with. See the Appendix and InTheWay-Book.com for more resources and organizations to contact.

Another point to bear in mind is patience. Speed of change toward DMM is probably not helpful. Is it important? Yes. Should we be deliberate, resolute? Absolutely. Fast? Not so much. Personally speaking, it took a full two years of practicing DMM for me to transition away from my default CAWKI methods and mindset— and this during a time when I wasn't actively in a staff position at a church. I've found this to be typical for others as well.

> Moving from a legacy church approach to a disciple-multiplying movement approach means you'll probably be off the edge of almost every ministry map you've ever used.

Remember: Disciple-making itself is not a microwave process, it is a crock-pot process (see *Contrast #8 – Growth Strategy: Fast vs. Slow*, chapter 6). It's more about focus and intentionality than productivity. Though you will make many mistakes in implementing DMM (that's how you will get better at it), at this point it's more about getting it "down" than getting it "done." Remember the power of multiplication: The process itself will bring results, so work the process with all diligence and wisdom.

Next Steps

Are you ready? Next comes the discussion about strategy.

11   Strategies and Implications

Things alter for the worse spontaneously, if they be not altered for the better designedly."

—Father Theodore Hesburgh

Now we turn from the "why" of DMM toward the "how." Assuming you've come out of the previous chapter having heard from God and confident with his call for you and/or your church to move forward in DMM, let's examine some high-level strategies on how to implement it.

The Wineskin Reality

In chapter 2, 'Paradigms and Perceptions', I introduced Jesus' parable of the wineskins to illustrate the challenges of changing a long-standing paradigm like the Western legacy church. I want to revisit the parable now, but this time with a view toward implementation strategy.

"No one tears a piece out of a new garment to patch an old one. Otherwise, they will have torn the new garment, and the patch from the new will not match the old. And no one pours new wine into old wineskins. Otherwise, the new wine will burst the skins; the wine will run out and the wineskins will be ruined. No, new wine must be poured into new wineskins. And no one after drinking old wine wants the new, for they say, 'The old is better.' " (Luke 5:36–39)

As I touched on in chapter 2, there are three things from Jesus' parable to keep in mind when considering implementing DMM:

1. The legacy church model is inappropriate for the purpose of multiplying disciple-making.
2. DMM and CAWKI are incompatible—their structure and functions are oriented around different priorities.
3. People who are comfortable in a legacy setting will not be comfortable with DMM.

There are two other things from the parable that shed light on building a DMM implementation strategy. First, the obvious point of Jesus' parable is that a choice for one or the other must be made. Many will be enticed to use a compromise strategy that implements some of the DMM principles and practices inside their CAWKI programs. This could include things like requiring the new disciples reached through DMM to also attend your Sunday services, or perhaps using a simple church approach in your small group structure without also changing their focus toward rapidly multiplying disciples. Taking the compromise approach may appear to make sense at first glance, but it's not a good idea. If I may, this is an attempt to hold on to the old approach as a safety net in case the attempt at DMM fails. It's a fear-based approach that will only come back to haunt you in the long run.

The second point is why the compromise approach won't work: The "skin" (i.e., the structure and programming) of the legacy church will not hold the "substance" of DMM ministry activity. The new wine will burst the old skin and both efforts will be lost, along with critical time, energy, resources and souls that go unsaved. The likely results of the compromise are predictable: The church will split. Those devoted to CAWKI will reject DMM and resent the leadership for attempting it. Those who embrace the new wine of DMM will be disillusioned and leave. Unity will become even more elusive and difficult to achieve. Failure is highly likely.

We should take great care in launching a disciple-making ministry effort from an existing legacy ministry organization. Because they are so different, we run the risk of not fully implementing a healthy disciple-making effort and dooming it to fail, while simultaneously damaging the existing ministry in the process.

The Strategy Big Picture

With the wineskin reality in view, I suggest two possible courses of action if you DO NOT believe the Lord is calling you to implement a DMM approach in your church (thanks to Chris Galanos and wigtakeDMM.com for identifying and unpacking these two options):

1. BLESS. You can do an incredible service to establishing a DMM ministry model simply by recognizing its validity and blessing those who are called to implement it. The more believers—and especially pastors and church leaders—in the West can support and encourage others to practice and prosper in discipleship multiplication, the more traction it will gain. Even if you and your church are not personally involved, your affirming words will go a long way to maintaining unity in the church in the West.[1]

2. RELEASE. If you have people in your church who are being called to practice disciple-multiplying movement strategies, you can take a step beyond blessing them (#1 above) and release them to the ministry, much as you would a missionary or church planter going out from your congregation. These people (who are called by the Holy Spirit to this work) will not be positioned

well if they remain in a legacy ministry model. They will very likely feel limited and probably frustrated. The act of releasing them affirms the Lord's call on their ministry. The release may involve prayer or even financial support, but it doesn't have to.[2]

If you *do*, however, believe the Lord is calling you toward a DMM ministry approach, there are three possible strategies for launching a disciple-multiplying movement I would invite you to consider:

1. START-UP. A new DMM church start-up is the most straight-forward strategy since it requires no effort in transitioning an existing church body.

2. TRANSITION. This strategy involves re-visioning the church and transitioning all the current ministries and programs to align with a DMM purpose.

3. PARALLEL. The final strategy option maintains the current legacy approach while creating a separate DMM strategy that runs along-side it.

Each of these three strategies is challenging in its own right, with distinct advantages and disadvantages in the context of your personal situation and existing ministry setting. Each will require faith and practice to execute well.

The Start-Up Strategy

This strategy should be viewed as a new church plant or start-up, except that the methods are completely different from starting a new legacy church plant.

Advantages
This approach has advantages in that there's no existing "wineskin" to deal with, so there's almost no organizational inertia to overcome.

Like a legacy church plant, the DMM church will be able to establish its own DNA from the outset.

One reality you'll need to grasp is that you'll have no identity to leverage or market. When you talk to people about a DMM-based church, virtually no one will understand it. Affiliation is important to our culture, so not being affiliated with anything will be received with skepticism. Being a DMM church provides even less of an affiliation than a normal CAWKI start-up. You should expect that your confident claims of affiliating with Jesus and the Bible will do little to alleviate caution and skepticism.

This identity issue sounds like a disadvantage, but it's actually helpful: You'll be starting fresh, and you'll use prayer and the power of your story and the love of Christ as your calling cards. These will set you apart.

Disadvantages

The start-up strategy does have some significant challenges. First, you'll have challenges with Christians from other churches who want to join you. They will likely have their own legacy experience and expectations that must be examined and managed. All the language you'll use to describe DMM is widely used in legacy church settings and has meanings unique to each person. You'll need to go the extra mile to fully define concepts like "making disciples," "being led by the Spirit," "surrendering our lives to Christ," "hearing from the Lord," and "obedience."

This approach has advantages in that there's no existing "wineskin" to deal with, so there's almost no organizational inertia to overcome.

Second, the Christians who join you may also be disenfranchised with their churches. This could be either good or bad, and probably even simultaneously good *and* bad (depending on their reasons for being disenfranchised).

Third, all these require allowing yourself a significant amount of time on the front end. Don't rush this step! Part of this is a vetting process: You want to ensure people are willing to hear and obey (the first and primary competency for a disciple-maker). You'll probably be tempted to put some people in ministry leadership positions based on their past ministry experience or Bible knowledge. Let people demonstrate faithfulness in small things before giving them responsibility in larger things—especially a leadership role. It also gives you time to discern if their dissatisfaction is sourced in a spirit of division or unwillingness to submit—which is even more caustic and damaging in a DMM ministry model.

The main reason for the extra time, however, is you'll need the time to disciple them. Remember: Everything you want them to do, you have to model for them first. They'll need to be trained, mentored, challenged, affirmed, corrected, steered, encouraged . . . and this simply takes time.

Case Study

1Body Church, Tampa, Florida (1body.church)

QUICK FACTS:

- STARTED: 2013 by Lee Wood, in response to being trained and mentored by mission strategist Curtis Sergeant.
- VISION: The name and vision for 1Body Ministries was inspired out of John 17:20–23: "I pray also for those who will believe in me … that they may be brought to complete unity. Then the world will know that you sent me and have loved them even as you have loved me." In 2016 the name was changed from 1Body Ministries to 1Body Church, with the purpose of launching and growing disciple-multiplying movements that transform communities until the whole world knows.

- STORY: Lee, a gifted apostle-evangelist and former CAWKI pastor, pressed forward with all diligence and started 67 groups in the first year with the mantra, "You can't screw this up!" Soon it became apparent this approach was ineffective, and, in fact, you can screw it up. So Lee stepped back from his role as the executive leader. A team of leaders with various gifts was formed around him and the ministry turned its attention from going fast and wide to going deep. The ministry responded to the Spirit's promptings to take on the identity of the church (instead of seeing itself as a para-church organization) and refocused its efforts on "pouring deeply into the few" who would obey Jesus. The effort has led to multiple generations of groups in the U.S., and has started streams of disciple-making efforts in various locations across the world that include well over ten generations.

The Transition Strategy

The second strategy is to transition an existing church by realigning all the church's current ministries and programs toward a disciple-multiplying movement purpose. This strategy is the most comprehensive when it comes to organizational change.

Advantages

The transition strategy allows for a clear vision and mission. It elevates disciple-making as the focus of the Christian life. It puts all the cards on the table, so to speak, and presents a clear and unmistakable vision the entire church must consider as the calling for their own lives. It is easier to lead an organization when the vision is clear and distinct—you know who you're called to be, and it leaves less room for interpretation.

When you complete the transition you will have a large group of disciples equipped and motivated toward accomplishing the Great Commission. Compared to the other two, this strategy (potentially) creates the largest leadership footprint to build on—assuming you choose leaders wisely, from those who both support the vision and those who have demonstrated obedience in the small things.

Disadvantages

The transition strategy is comprehensive in almost every way, and will dominate the life and focus of the church for a significant length of time. It requires a great deal of planning in advance, as you will need clear ideas about how to manage each part of the church's programs over what will likely be a multi-year, phased project.

Of the three strategies, this is the most disruptive on the congregation. Many congregants, staff, and lay leaders will be disillusioned and leave because they favor the "old wine." Many will fail to understand and be confused. You should expect that a significant percentage of your congregation will not embrace the new DMM approach and leave for another church. Don't be surprised if this is on the order of ninety percent or greater.

This strategy requires you to be solidly and securely positioned in your leadership status. You'll receive a full spectrum of reaction, from support and encouragement on one side to resistance and backlash on the other—though likely more of the latter, and that from people you won't anticipate.

This strategy requires you to be solidly and securely positioned in your leadership status. You'll receive a full spectrum of reaction, from support and encouragement on one side to resistance and backlash on the other.

The transition strategy also requires a lot of work up front to cast vision and secure buy-in. Anticipate lots of time for meetings and lengthy conversations. Prepare yourself and the leadership team to be long on patience and grace, even as you also demonstrate conviction and clarity. You'll want to be optimistic and visionary, yet at the same time realistic about the scope of the changes and the disruption.

As you might expect, the church will likely experience significant fiscal changes as many people will reduce or eliminate their giving. Depending on the size of the church, the staffing model you are currently using will likely change significantly. A DMM model doesn't require as many full-time paid staff, so many of the staff can transition to part-time or bivocational status.

You'll need a clear path for navigating through the entire transition, which could take multiple years. At different points you may feel distracted as you sustain CAWKI programs with one hand and train and release people for DMM ministry with the other.

Case Study

Experience Life Church, Lubbock, Texas (experiencelifenow.com). eLife Church's experience is told through the eyes of the founding Sr. Pastor, Chris Galanos, in his book *From Megachurch to Multiplication: A Church's Journey Toward Movement.*[3]

QUICK FACTS:

- STARTED: 2007 by Lead Pastor Chris Galanos as a new, attractional legacy church.
- VISION: The church's original vision was to reach 10,000 people in ten years. But the DMM approach inspired Chris and his team to ask God to help them reach not just 10,000 people, but instead to reach 1,000,000 people.
- STORY: The church started in Chris' living room with 12 people and grew to over 8,000 in weekly attendance (ten campuses) in ten years, with 13,000+ professions of faith and 6,000+

baptisms. In asking God what was in store for the next ten years, Chris read David Garrison's book *Church Planting Movements*[4] where he was exposed to DMM strategy. He and his team began a multi-year process of implementing DMM internally, eventually announcing the change in vision to the church at its ten-year anniversary. They trained fifty-four people in the initial wave of DMM, then began transitioning the programmatic aspects of the church over the next year to align with a DMM approach to include three major elements: prayer, testimony, and training. They now have groups in the third generation.

The Parallel Strategy

The third strategy is to keep the current legacy ministry intact while creating a DMM strategy that runs simultaneously alongside it. I call this the parallel strategy, which is a "both-and" rather than an "either-or" strategy. Some might see this as a sort of church plant, except A) the new daughter church will have a completely different ministry approach, and B) it will remain under the leadership and support of the parent church.

The key factor that makes this strategy work is the two approaches— legacy and DMM—do not interact. In other words, the legacy side of the ministry maintains a "come" approach and provides a way for people who view church as a Sunday morning congregational event to connect. At the same time, those who participate in the DMM side of the ministry are able to operate outside of the programmatic elements of the legacy ministry (in a true "go" approach).

Remembering the wineskin parable, you should avoid the temptation of expecting people to participate in both the DMM and the CAWKI ministry structures at the same time. The separation should be maintained. In fact—as drastic as this may sound—you should consider avoiding even the public association of the two efforts. By this I mean that the people you'll be reaching through the DMM efforts will be confused as they try to reconcile the different identities. To be most effective, the people reached through DMM need their prime associations to be with Jesus and the person discipling them.

Think of the DMM effort as sending out missionaries into the field, except that the field is in the same community as your existing congregation. If managed well, the two models will not compete with each other. The DMM model won't require much (if any) staff resources, money, facilities, programming support, etc. Its primary needs are authorization, blessing, training, and encouragement. The people who come to your legacy ministry programming likely won't find the DMM approach very appealing. Likewise, the people you reach in a DMM will likely not be comfortable trying to integrate into the legacy ministry.

Advantages

Properly managed, the parallel strategy allows both ministries to function underneath the same leadership umbrella. Organizationally-speaking, it creates an R&D effort to run autonomously without disrupting operations in the original legacy organization.

> Think of the DMM effort as sending out missionaries into the field, except that the field is in the same community as your existing congregation.

This it is not often employed, but neither is it unheard of. Back in the 1960s the Lockheed Corporation used this strategy to create a separate, autonomous division called the Skunk Works that focused on secret "black" projects. This team created the famous SR-71 "Blackbird," a high-speed reconnaissance aircraft so advanced that in thirty-four years not a single plane was lost to enemy action. And the day it was retired from service it set four new speed records. This approach was also famously used by Carol Shelby as a part of the Ford Motor Company's efforts to win the historic 24 Hours of Le Mans auto race from 1966–1969.

Disadvantages

The church's leadership will need to be unified in the strategy and be impartially supportive of the purpose for each ministry. In essence, the leadership will have to walk in both worlds simultaneously—with integrity, and without compromise. As a leader, you'll have (in a sense) two favorite children; if you favor one at the expense of the other you will not be able to successfully lead this strategy.

From a management standpoint, you'll need to be nimble enough to switch focus from one ministry (and its priorities and methods) to the other and back again, sometimes in a moment's notice. In my experience as a leadership coach, this is not easy to do and not every leader is practically capable of pulling this off. It's not a matter of having the mental horsepower, it's more a matter of how God has "wired" each of us. Some of us prefer a single focus and calling, while others are able to switch between initiatives without compromise.

Another consideration is that senior organizational leaders should establish capable leaders for each ministry in order to delegate leadership to them and let them run with it. This will minimize the "switching" challenge mentioned above. But more importantly it allows you to maintain a strategic view of the direction and operation of both ministries. Of course, it also requires capable leaders to be able delegate to.

Case Study

Shoal Creek Community Church, Kansas City, Missouri (shoalcreek.org)

Roy Moran, lead pastor of Shoal Creek, is the author of *Spent Matches: Igniting the Signal Fire for the Spiritually Dissatisfied.*[5]

QUICK FACTS:

- STARTED: Shoal Creek's core group formed in the spring of 1993 and launched services in 1995 as a seeker-friendly church start-up modeled after Willow Creek Community Church.

- VISION: The church's mission is to "make Jesus accessible." Ultimately, this starts the rebuilding process that heals people, creating connected communities where the redeeming power of Jesus moves through relationships and remakes our broken world.

- STORY: Shoal Creek started off with a vision to reach the 300,000 people within a thirty-minute drive from their location. After eight years they were able to move to another property. At this point Roy read Ronald Allen's *The Spontaneous Expansion of the Church and the Causes Which Hinder It*. Roy began to see the limitations of his vision: There was no way their 1,200-seat facility with 450 parking spaces could accommodate and disciple that many people. At year eleven with 800 in attendance, the church adopted what they call a "hybrid" strategy that allows them "to make disciples at viral rates, irrespective of traditionally trained leaders and adequate facilities, and to be a church with an aggressive heart to reach those not yet vitally connected with their heavenly Father through His Son."[6] They currently operate both "come" and "go" as separate ministry strategies. They maintain their Sunday morning programming and aggressively ask people to invite their unchurched friends, while also training and equipping people to make disciple-making disciples in groups out in the community and not overtly tied to the visible church.

Strategy Implications for Leaders

Any of the three strategies above will have implications you need to be aware of. There are certain assumptions you must intentionally challenge when you consider launching a DMM ministry.

Many of these topics were touched on in 'Part 2: Contrasts', but it's helpful to point them out again in the context of creating an implementation strategy. This segment is a "count the cost" effort when it comes to your leadership: If you're not comfortable with these implications in your ministry setting, my encouragement is to spend more time and seek wise counsel before pressing ahead.

Move Away From Positional Influence
The best DMM leaders don't rely on their position as pastor and all that comes with it, like education, speaking ability, winsome personality, experience, or Bible knowledge. Those all have a place, of course, but they are not the driving factors. Instead, their greatest influence comes through modeling the basic commands of Christ, and immediately and deliberately empowering others to do the same—so those empowered aren't dependent upon the leader.

The implications of this are significant: Because discipleship is such an intensely relational process, it's actually more "caught" than "taught." So leaders must be prepared to model every aspect of obedience to Christ. If you're not a disciple-making disciple you can't influence and apprentice others to be one, no matter how well you intellectually understand it—you can't give away what you don't have.

Pace and Schedule
DMM is a marathon, not a sprint; a crock pot rather than a microwave. Expect it to be slower than you're probably comfortable with. In our experience, it is common for people with a legacy church background

(particularly church staff) to take two years to fully transition from the CAWKI ministry paradigm to a disciple-multiplying movement paradigm. The changes are significant and deep-seated, and should not be underestimated.

Also related to pace is that you must fight the urge to move fast, primarily in the initial phases. Effective disciple-making is slow and unimpressive for the first few years. When you focus on numbers of people, numbers of groups, etc., it doesn't look like much. It's only when you get to several generations that it gains noticeable momentum.

Don't get caught in the temptation to be impatient and artificially speed up the process for the sake of increasing a perceived productivity. I hear many DMM practitioners in America mention the urge to increase their ministry metrics (how many groups, people, etc.). We are so conditioned in the West to think more and faster are better. Yet in disciple-making, it's exactly opposite: fewer and slower are better. If you're like most, you probably don't realize how deep-seated this tendency is.

> If you're not a disciple-making disciple, you can't influence and apprentice others to be one, no matter how well you intellectually understand it—you can't give away what you don't have.

Developing Leaders

You'll likely have many who will want to lead—and on the surface appear adequate to lead. But shy away from giving leadership responsibility based upon time in the faith, Bible or theological knowledge, their role in the marketplace, etc. Instead, you'll want to look for faithfulness to hear, obey and follow Jesus' examples (see 2 Tim. 2:2), along with a servant attitude. You'll want to establish this pattern and stick with it: If you compromise and give leadership responsibility to those who aren't capable disciple-makers it will slow the growth of your ministry, likely setting you back years.

Reduce the frequency of teaching venues in developing leaders (especially Bible teaching). You'll have lots of opportunity to teach the Bible organically as you walk with people in a discipleship relationship. Besides that, God will be revealing Scripture passages to them he wants them to learn—let the Holy Spirit be the teacher and let your role shift from teacher to mentor.

Increase the priority of application-based training—which is different than teaching. Training is more about giving people a little knowledge, letting them practice, then debriefing on how it went and developing accountability on how to continue improving. Discipleship is something you do (not something you know), so if you don't practice it you won't get any better.

Target APEST Team Development

When it comes to the five Ephesians 4 APEST giftings (apostles, prophets, evangelists, shepherds, and teachers), most legacy churches develop the last two: shepherds and teachers. A successful DMM will require you to recognize, validate, authorize, and equip leaders of all five. Help people understand their gift(s), how to use them, and how to operate in unity with each other.

The key with APEST comes when all the gifts actively collaborate as a team. This is a challenge, because it requires mutual submission. North American Christians are so accustomed to the hierarchical approach that mutual submission to others in community is often a foreign concept.

Decentralized Ministry Management

The typical management approach in a legacy setting is much more centralized control, where there are strict approval processes and expectations. You'll need to transition from this "controlling" mindset to an "empowering" mindset where managing groups and leaders is more about equipping and releasing, then support- ing, monitoring, and coaching for improvement and quality. Trust that dedicated, committed, engaged disciples will hear from and respond to the leading of the Holy Spirit and God's word.

> We are so conditioned in the West to think more and faster are better. Yet in disciple-making it's exactly opposite: fewer and slower are better.

Be Relentless About Multiplication

In implementing a DMM approach, it's highly likely that people will want to settle for being the distributed the church in smaller congregations. It's easy for legacy Christians to assume that meeting in homes equates to obeying Jesus' command to "go," since they aren't tied to the church facility or programming any more. If this settling happens, the drive for discipleship multiplication usually dies on the vine.

The simple but nuanced truth is that miniaturizing the CAWKI approach and making it more intimate and casual in an off-campus, home environment is not multiplicative discipleship. It may be a wonderful experience, but unless it creates new streams of disci-ple-making outside the existing relationship network it will never lead to movement.

This is the same dynamic facing the legacy church today that is distributing due to COVID (as I mentioned in *A COVID-19 Observation* [page 79]). Time will ultimately tell, but as of this writing there are many churches and individual believers looking to shift to a house church model, believing it to be more suitable for discipleship. But the shift in location and setting alone will not facilitate disciple-making.

As a leader, you must be relentless about multiplication as the fruit of the strategy. Pray over it. Model it. Cast vision for it. Train it. Hold people accountable to it. Never forget: Without multiplication—where individual believers are equipped and engaged in making disciples that make other disciples—we'll never see the Great Commission completed.

Seven Things We've Learned

No matter what strategy you go with, I can virtually guarantee you will be stretched and challenged. As stated previously, in many ways you will feel somewhat "lost;" this journey will be unlike any previous ministry experience you've had before. You'll probably be surprised at how much you have to "unlearn" before you can learn to make more and better disciples. Don't let this alarm you; you aren't alone.

Our experience at 1Body Church—both painful and rewarding—has taught us some key principles that have continually proven themselves to be true. We affectionately call them "The 7 Things We've Learned in 7 Years." They all defy our natural inclinations: We must intentionally press against the natural in the power of the Spirit.

1. **You take care of depth of your ministry; God will take care of the breadth of your ministry.** Go deep, not wide. Going deep with people is slower. Think quality, not quantity. Trust God for the growth as he sees fit, not as what seems opportunistic.

2. **Pour deeply into the few who will obey no matter the cost.** There are few faithful ones who will surrender to Jesus and follow his narrow path. Look for them; and when you find them, call them. Don't just share the gospel with them, live it with them. You can only do that with a few, so switch from an addition mindset (share gospel and invite many) to a multiplication mindset (make disciples who obey Jesus).

3. **Keep doing what you're doing, you'll get better!** I promise you: You will fail! Don't be discouraged, keep practicing by doing.

4. **Obey the Lord personally and train others intentionally.** You can't give away what you don't have. You can't reproduce what's not already being practiced in your own life.

5. **Simple things grow, simple things multiply.** You don't get extra points for being complex. Complexity won't reproduce, it slows things down and adds no value in the long run. Besides, simple is way easier.

6. **It's always relational before it's organizational.** Don't start with organization and structure. Don't think "program." Instead, think "friend." Focus on relationships first and let organization develop organically. At every level; always, always, always.

7. **Connect, communicate, and collaborate.** There is power and unity in the broad and practical connection of the church, communicating frequently and collaborating freely—where no individual segment either receives glory nor suffers alone. The worldliness of the Western culture motivates and incentivizes isolation and self-promotion; we must actively resist it.

> This journey will be unlike any previous ministry experience you've had before. You'll probably be surprised at how much you have to "unlearn" before you can learn to make more and better disciples. Don't let this alarm you; you aren't alone.

Each of the "7 Things" has come through hard and sometimes painful lessons. But by God's grace and his ability to redeem our mistakes, we've learned so much about practicing a DMM-model of ministry in the culture of the U.S. We continue to learn as we continue to trust God in the process and trust that he will continue to guide us forward.

12 Changing the Church

It is impossible for a man to learn what he thinks he already knows.

—Epictetus

No matter the strategy choice, the change effort should be managed well for maximum impact. This chapter highlights some of the major components of organizational change from a leadership perspective, as well as things the congregation will experience as it embraces a disciple-multiplying movement strategy.

The Nature of Change

Change is one of the more difficult challenges an organization will face, so it is one of the most vital of leadership responsibilities. Change management is an organizational leadership discipline that many marketplace leaders are trained in and leverage on a regular basis. But in my experience, precious few ministry organizations or leaders are aware of the key components of change management.

You should not implement a transition to a DMM ministry model without an awareness of organizational change principles. If this is a new topic for you, I suggest getting up to speed on the issues and processes involved. I highly recommend *Leading Change*, by John Kotter,[1] one of the foremost experts on the subject. This book is written in a business context but the principles addressed are applicable for a ministry organizational context.

The Change Formula

As a starting point, I've found this formula to be a helpful way to think about change:

$$D_{SQ} + K_{BW} + K_{FS} > I$$

Where:

- D_{SQ} = Dissatisfaction with the Status Quo
- K_{BW} = Knowledge of a Better Way
- K_{FS} = Knowledge of First Steps to take
- I = Inertia (resisting the change and keeping the status quo in place)

Change can only occur when the level of D_{SQ}, combined with K_{BW} and K_{FS} exceeds the level of Inertia resisting the change. Let's look at each of the four elements to understand why this is so.

D_{SQ}

Dissatisfaction with the status quo is the single biggest factor in motivating change in people or in an organization. If people are satisfied with the status quo there's simply no reason for them to change. The call to change will essentially fall on deaf ears, and they will continue to do what they've always done. On the other hand, when people are dissatisfied the atmosphere is ripe for change.

You should recognize that your personal level of dissatisfaction—as the change champion—will very likely be higher than others in the congregation (at least at the outset). You will have to develop specific ways to objectively measure levels of dissatisfaction at the various strategic change levels. This is an important step; one you don't want to swing and miss on.

Once measured, the next challenge will be raising the levels of D_{SQ} in everyone else to match your own. You'll want to use your leadership influence to broaden the D_{SQ} so it's shared by as many people as possible—but especially all the stakeholders.

Once the change is initiated, the leadership challenge shifts toward maintaining the D_{SQ} throughout the change process. It is the fire that fuels the change effort. As people go through the mental, emotional, practical, social, and—above all—spiritual changes, you'll want to ensure this fire never goes out.

K_{BW}

This book presents the Knowledge of a Better Way (K_{BW}). Some additional resources are included in Appendix A. You should do your due diligence in clarifying the K_{BW}, since you'll be both invited and challenged to defend the change. You'll want to be able to clearly articulate what the better way is.

But you should also recognize it's easy to over-do this. You can expend too much time and energy trying to answer every question and researching every possible scenario. My encouragement is to spend enough time in the K_{BW} to be competent and convicted, then move forward in faith.

K_{FS}

K_{FS} is just that: first steps. Like K_{BW}, determining K_{FS} involves a component of faith. So don't be afraid if you don't have a detailed outline for a ten-year plan. You just want to know enough to be confident about where you want to go and how to get the change initiated. K_{FS} resources are also included in Appendix A, but I would highly recommend leveraging live training and connecting with DMM practitioner organizations that can serve as mentors for you, like Biglife,

24:14, New Generations, No Place Left, Beyond, E3 Partners, and Team Expansion.

I

The level of inertia resisting change will be unique to you and your church. You alone know how your firmly-seated traditions, affiliations, sacred cows, values, heritage, history, etc. will be threatened by moving

Change can only occur when the level of Dissatisfaction combined with the Knowledge of a Better Way and Knowledge of First Steps exceeds the level Inertia resisting the change.

toward a DMM approach. Never underestimate the emotional attachment people have to these elements—especially for older congregations where they've been in place for a long time. If you miss or underestimate the chunks that make up the inertia, you will lose credibility, you'll alienate yourself from the people you are leading, your new vision and strategy will be rejected, and you simply will not be able to implement change.

Making the Change Formula Work

Here are a few things to consider related to implementing the change formula.

Pace

You'll notice one thing not included in the formula: a time frame. Pace or rate of change is important but will vary from one organization to the next. The main goal is to keep the change moving; maintain momentum and don't let it stall.

There are many factors, but the main thing is the rate of change has to be correlated with the elements of the formula. For instance, if the D_{SQ} is high, the church will have a greater sense of urgency and will welcome a faster rate of change. In contrast, if the D_{SQ} is lower, the church will be a bit more cautious and a high rate of change will cause people to pump the breaks on change.

Change At the Major Organizational Levels

There are groups within the church with unique roles and levels of engagement that must be considered and managed differently. First is the natural size groups, from individual, to family unit, to (perhaps) geographical or neighborhood groupings, to congregational. What will it look like to communicate with each group and deal with change issues at their level?

Another level to consider is the stakeholder levels. You'll want to identify each grouping of people who have a perceived stake in the organization. For instance, the church staff, the core leaders (like the church elder or deacon board), the key volunteer teams, the church members, and the rest of the congregation. Each group of stakeholders has a different level of engagement and perceived level of "skin in the game." Each must be evaluated and approached commensurate with how the change will impact them.

Also, you'll want to sequence your interaction with each group to maximize their involvement in the change. For example, engaging your key leadership early will allow you to gauge the response to the change, get honest feedback and suggestions on how to proceed, and—most importantly—to include them as change agents in rolling out the change to the other groups in the church.

Dealing With Resistance

There's no way around it: Change creates resistance. The most obvious comment here is simply expect it; or more aptly, embrace it. Don't fall into the trap of judging people because they push back on the change.

Resistance is not (necessarily) a sign of rejection of the vision, it is simply an indication of the gap between where the church is now and where it will be once the change is complete. The wider the gap, the more resistance you can anticipate.

And that's the biggest favor you can do for yourself: Anticipate resistance. Consider each group and level of stakeholders from the perspective of what they stand to lose, what they may/may not understand, how the change will impact them, how it might threaten them, what they need to know to have their concerns addressed appropriately, and how you can turn their resistance in your favor.

Communicate, Communicate, Communicate

There's almost no way to over-communicate during a significant change process. Increasing information and personal connection between key change agents and the church will smooth over differences and reveal opportunities to deal with issues you didn't anticipate or resistance that may be brewing just under the surface. You'll want to make sure church leaders are as accessible as possible during the change.

Spiritual Attack

I encourage you to be vigilant in watching for spiritual attack during the change. Organizations are most vulnerable during times of change, and the issues that arise during change are easy targets for spiritual attack.

Remember: Satan is an enemy, opposing any effort that strengthens the body of Christ, so prepare in advance for ways he might disrupt your efforts. Use the "full armor of God" in Ephesians 6:10–20 to oppose him.

Here's a quick list I call the "10 Ds" that highlights his tactics (how he operates) and goals (outcomes he's working toward):

1. DISTRACT—He will attempt to get us to focus on things that are ancillary and not a priority.

2. DIVERT—He will work to get us to detour from the path God lays out for us.

3. DISREGARD—He tries to get us to dismiss God's faithfulness and provision, and to move us to depend on other things (the world, our own capacities, etc.).

4. DISCOURAGE—He wants us to be in a place where we are lacking hope, where we lose conviction, confidence, resiliency, and our ability to stand strong in our faith.

5. DECEIVE—He's very skilled at telling half-truths, where we embracing the truth part not realizing it's hiding a subtle lie.

6. DOUBT—He schemes to get us to distrust God's will, intention, promises and character.

7. DENY—His most damaging work begins when we start denying the truth we believe in; once we lose our tether to truth, it becomes much easier for him to do his work.

8. DISOBEY—He relishes when we choose not to follow Jesus' commands.

9. DIVIDE—He constantly tries to drive a wedge into our key relationships: our spouses and family members, fellow believers, other churches, and even between us and God.

10. DEATH—His ultimate intent is to steal, kill and destroy; and all his tactics are aimed at this outcome.

As you survey the stories of the Scriptures you'll see how these tactics were deployed with God's people. You may notice that the "10 Ds" tend to build on each other. The first three or four are relatively minor and subtle. These covert actions aren't as recognizable, and he's often just sowing seeds that will later blossom into larger vulnerabilities. Once he finds inroads into our hearts and minds using them, he then raises the stakes and becomes more overt. The final four are the most damaging, and often these are the most visible.

A major change initiative in your church like implementing a DMM strategy will create lots of opportunity for these. Prepare yourself and your church in advance.

Identity vs. Methodology

The final and perhaps most important change consideration is that operating within a disciple-multiplying movement is—at its core—an issue of identity, not methodology. This is true for the leadership as well as the church as a whole.

You can't function effectively in a disciple-multiplying movement approach—at any leadership level—unless you see yourself as a disciple whose primary calling and function is to obey Christ's teachings in discipling others. This must begin with you, personally; in your own life.

A disciple-multiplying movement approach is not simply a new method to try. It is not something you add to your current life; it is something you reorient your life around. It alone becomes your priority that provides context to everything else and all other priorities in life.

Gulp...

Don't approach this as a fad, a new fill-in-the-gap method, or quick-response program to deploy; that will only set you up for failure. The level of DSQ will be highest when the congregation comes to the bottom line of identity. This is the level where personal and corporate values exist: When we realize who we are, and who we're supposed to be.

Not to make this trite or trivial, but this is the point in *The Lion King* where Mufasa reminds Simba that he has forgotten who he is. This realization motivates Simba to take on the responsibility of the leadership and take on his arch-enemy Scar. This is more than a good Disney story, it is rooted in our most basic psychology as a part of how we were made in God's image and in the identity Jesus gave us through being his followers. Our identity is given to us from God, and our greatest success and fulfillment come when we live out that identity.

A major component of this in disciple-making is that our identity is fully found in Christ. Many Christians embrace this intellectually, doctrinally. My experience is that a minority of believers in the West embrace this practically, experientially. The implication of our identity in Christ is that our life is not our own. This means we willingly and trustingly give up control of our lives: no agenda, no self-driven autonomy, or self-determined attitude. This surrender is so complete that we have one approach: Do what the Holy Spirit

> A disciple-multiplying movement approach is not simply a new method to try. It is not something you add to your current life; it is something you reorient your life around. It alone becomes your priority that provides context to everything else and all other priorities in life.

tells us, when he tells us to do it. Here there is no fear, no pride, no selfish motives, no conceit. Only peace and security in abiding in Jesus.

Operating in this mindset will radically change how you see yourself, how you see others, and how you call others to come with you as you follow Jesus. Two resources that personally helped shape this perspective on identity are Steve Smith's *Spirit Walk*[2] and Curtis Sergeant's *The Only One*.[3]

The Final Word: Unity

Without question, transitioning your church to a DMM-centered ministry model is a big deal. But looming even larger is the realization that DMM is a much bigger issue than a single local church in the West. Your local church's investment in DMM is a part of a global movement. This is your opportunity to connect—practically and missionally—to what God is doing on a much larger scale, at a level we've not seen in the history of the church before now.

Right now, movements are encroaching on the last of the peoples furthest from the gospel. These unreached/unengaged people groups (UPGS) have never even heard the name of Jesus Christ—not even once. Yet organizations and coalitions like 24:14 are working together, using DMM as a centralizing strategy to penetrate these once unbreachable strongholds. These efforts include people from a broad spectrum of organizational traditions that have put aside their differences in perspective and methodologies to work collaboratively on the one mission Christ gave us: Go and make disciples of all nations. Instead of asking, "What can we do," they are asking "What must be done?" and then doing it together, with sacrificial urgency.

Believers of all walks of life and in every corner of the globe are faithfully making disciples. Many are seeing incredible fruit despite very little resources. Many are operating under daily hardships and the threat of persecution. Many others are suffering and dying for the sake of the gospel—and most churches in the U.S. have zero awareness of what they are facing. DMM can and should be a part of raising the awareness. For more insight on what's happening with persecuted brothers and sisters in Christ and how this can be a part of your vision-casting, I highly recommend Dominic Sputo's *Heirloom Love: Authentic Christianity for This Age of Persecution.*[4] It's also available in a small group study format.[5]

DMM is the ministry equalizer, the great church connector. Using this approach allows us to genuinely experience unity at a level the church hasn't seen since the early centuries of its existence. Local churches, all with varied theological and doctrinal positions, can partner around multiplying disciples without compromising their foundational convictions.

Think about the impact of this: All the churches in the West that call upon the name of Jesus have been operating in a divided state for their entire history, and now we have the opportunity to be united and actually accomplish the mission Jesus gave us! The apostle Paul implored the Ephesian church to "make every effort to keep the unity of the spirit through the bond of peace" (Eph. 4:2). We have fallen short of this imperative. But more importantly than focusing on how we've fallen short is seizing the opportunity that awaits us moving forward, to God's glory.

All the churches in the West that call upon the name of Jesus have been operating in a divided state for their entire history, and now we have the opportunity to be united and actually accomplish the mission Jesus gave us!

I ask you to pray about this and let the Holy Spirit guide you. You have an opportunity to cast vision to your church with a message they've probably never even considered. When the time comes for conversations about your church's vision and mission, when you sit with the stakeholders about the dissatisfaction with your church's status quo, this is your opportunity to call them to the greatest degree of change the church in the West has ever seen.

Today, if you hear his voice...

May God speed and bless the work of your hands, to great fruitfulness for His name's sake. Amen and amen!

Appendices

See this section for organizations and resources
to help you understand and embrace a DMM strategy

Appendix A: DMM Resources

DMM Reading and Tools

Books, Articles

Addison, Steve. *Movements That Change the World: Five Keys to Spreading the Gospel* (Downers Grove: InterVarsity Press, 2011).

———. *Pioneering Movements: Leadership That Multiplies Disciples and Churches* (Downers Grove: InterVarsity Press, 2015).

———. *The Rise and Fall of Movements: A Roadmap for Leaders* (100Movements Publishing, 2019).

Allen, Roland. *The Spontaneous Expansion of the Church and the Causes that Hinder It* (Eugene, OR: Wipf and Stock Publishers, 1962).

Esler, Ted. "Two Church Planting Paradigms." *International Journal of Frontier Missiology*, Summer 2013.

Galanos, Chris. *From Megachurch to Multiplication: A Church's Journey Toward Movement*. Experience Life, 2018.

———. wigtakeDMM.com. This is a series of articles explaining key steps and information related to DMM. It is a good companion resource to Galanos' *From Megachurch to Multiplication*.

Garrison, David. *Church Planting Movements: How God Is Redeeming a Lost World* (Midlothian: WIGTake Resources, 2004).

Hunt, Dave. *A Revolution in Church Multiplication in East Africa: Transformational Leaders Develop A Self-Sustainable Model of Rapid Church Multiplication*, dissertation submitted to the faculty of Bakke University in candidacy for degree of doctor of ministry.

Lucas, Doug. *More Disciples: A Guide to Becoming and Multiplying Followers of Jesus* (Monument: WIGTake Resources, 2019).

Moran, Roy. *Spent Matches: Igniting the Signal Fire for the Spiritually Dissatisfied* (Nashville: Thomas Nelson, 2015).

Robertson, Patrick and Watson, David. *Father Glorified* (Nashville: Thomas Nelson, 2013).

Sergeant, Curtis. *The Only One: Living Fully In, By, and for God* (Littleton: William Carey Library Publishing, 2018).

Smith, Steve. *The Spirit Walk: The Extraordinary Power of Acts for Ordinary People* (Kingwood: 2414 Ventures, 2018).

Smith, Steve and Kai, Ying. *T4T: A Discipleship Re-Revolution* (Monument: WIGTake Resources, 2011).

Trousdale, Jerry. *Miraculous Movements: How Hundreds of Thousands of Muslims Are Falling in Love With Jesus* (Nashville: Thomas Nelson, 2012).

Trousdale, Jerry and Sunshine, Glenn. *The Kingdom Unleashed* (DMM Library, 2018).

Watson, David and Watson, Paul. *Contagious Disciple-Making: Leading Others on a Journey of Discovery* (Nashville: Thomas Nelson, 2014).

Apps and Online Tools

Discovery Group – An app for use in facilitating a Discovery Group, available on Android and iOS devices.

DiscipleMakingMovements.com – Website dedicated to exploring, learning, practicing, and connecting with others globally who are engaged in the lifestyle of multiplying disciples often referred to as discovery model. Sponsored by New Generations.

Disciple.Tools (disciple.tools) – An online site with combined features of a CRM, group- and leadership generation tracking, saturation strategy and mapping, and media to movement software for connecting online seekers with offline disciple makers.

Gen Mapper (noplaceleft.tools) – This site allows you to create and map out the generations of disciple-making groups and/or relationships. Sponsored by NoPlaceLeft.

Joshua Project (https://joshuaproject.net) – This site documents the major ethnic groups around the world, where they are, and to what degree the gospel has penetrated.

DMM Training
Metacamp (metacamp.org).
Zume (zumeproject.com).
Module 1 – Disciples Making Disciples (see Biglife or 1Body church).
Multiplication Concepts. This is a series of instructional videos featuring missions strategist Curtis Sergeant. To access, go to YouTube and search for "Multiplication Concepts Curtis Sergeant."
Disciple-Making Movements Learning Community (DMLC), https://shoalcreek.org/wp-content/uploads/2014/04/DMLCver2.pdf.
Engage! is an interactive course designed to give churches and individuals experience in expanding and extending God's Kingdom by facilitating Discovery Bible Studies (DBS) and initiating a DMM. For more information contact: jking@finalcommand.org.
Jonathan Training – This is a basic training on DMM principles conducted by Team Expansion. For more info, go to: http://teamexpansion.org/trainings.

DMM Practitioner Churches and Organizations
1Body Church, Tampa, Florida (1body.church). See the website for a number of training resources (1body.church/manual-docs) or to contact us (1body.church/connect/contact).
24:14 (2414now.net).
Accelerate (accelerateteams.org).
Beyond (beyond.org).
Biglife (big.life).
New Generations (newgenerations.org).

Contagious Disciple Making (contagiousdisciplemaking.com).

E3 Partners (e3partners.org).

Experience Life Church (experiencelifenow.com).

No Place Left (noplaceleft.net).

Shoal Creek Community Church (shoalcreek.org). Gather a group for DMM coaching. Sessions are two hours for nine weeks to explore the ten mind-shifts needed to get from ministry to movement. Contact Moran (roy.moran@shoalcreek.org).

Team Expansion (teamexpansion.org).

Appendix B: 3/3^{rds} Group Meeting Format

You can think of the 3/3^{rds} Group Meeting Format as a framework for any kind of conversation or agenda for a Bible-based discovery meeting. This format can be used whenever followers of Jesus meet. It is flexible: It can be extended over multiple hours or it can be done simply in 30 minutes.

Facilitation should be shared in the group (i.e., don't have the same person facilitating the group every week). The goal is not to exchange knowledge, but to discover God's truth, hear his direction and establish accountability around obeying what he reveals. It is important that everyone participates, and try to let the interaction flow naturally (e.g., try to avoid going around the room in an ordered fashion).

The format is broken into three segments ("thirds"): "look back" on events since the previous meeting to highlight and celebrate how God has worked, "look up" to hear from God as we read and discuss his Word, and "look forward" to hear from God and commit to obeying what he reveals to us.

First "3rd" – Look Back

Care and Worship.
Share a meal together. Interact around how everyone's personal relationship with God has been. If anyone is struggling, pray for him/her, and stay after to care for that person. Spend some time worshiping God through singing and prayer, using any spiritual gifts God has given your church.

Check-Up [never skip]
Questions to Ask:

- How have you obeyed what you have learned?
- Who have you trained in what you have learned?
- With whom have you shared your story (i.e., testimony) or God's story (i.e., the gospel)?

Vision [never skip]

Remind the group what their vision is every week: to multiply disciples and groups/churches. Share a story from the Bible, a personal story, or song to encourage one another to share Jesus with others, start new groups/churches, and help others do the same. Or use one of the following Bible passages to get started: Matt. 28:18–20, Luke 10:1–11, Luke 19:1–10, Acts 1:8.

Second "3rd" – Look Up

Pray.

Talk with God simply and briefly. Ask God to teach you this week's passage.

Read and Discuss.

Read this week's passage, then ask:
- What did you like about this passage?
- What did you not like (or what did you find challenging) about this passage? Read this week's passage again, then ask:
- What does this passage teach us about God?
- What does this passage teach us about people?

Third "3rd" – Look Forward

Pray, listen, and make commitments [never skip]
Allow a brief time (3–5 minutes) for everyone in the group to pray silently for God to show them how to answer these questions:

- How will you obey this passage?
- Who will you train with this passage?
- With whom will you share your story or God's story?

After the time of prayer and reflection, each person shares with the group what God revealed to them. Have someone write down each person's response and what they will commit to do in the coming week to obey.

Practice [never skip]
In groups of two or three, take a few minutes to practice what you have committed to do in the questions above. For example:

- Role-play a difficult conversation
- Create a specific plan or steps about how you will face a temptation
- Practice teaching today's passage, or
- Practice sharing the gospel.

After you are done, pray with your partner(s) and ask God to prepare the hearts of the people who will be hearing about Jesus this week. Ask Him to give you the strength to be obedient to your commitments.

Group Meeting Principles

Small
Keep groups small. Start groups around circles of relationships, people who already know each other. Meet where these people already gather,

for example in a home, café, or under a tree. With a larger group, divide into sub-groups of three, four or five people if you are short on time.

Everyone Learns to Grow On Their Own
In the group, everyone learns to grow by doing the following on their own:

1. Tell others about Jesus
2. Learn from the Bible
3. Talk with God and listen to Him
4. Help and encourage other believers
5. Boldly face persecution and hard times.

Consider Everyone a Potential Disciple-Maker
View everyone as a potential disciple-maker, regardless of whether they have trusted Jesus or not. Leaders do not require formal training or authorization. Anyone can lead the discussion, and in fact everyone in the group should lead the discussion at some point.

Obey and Train
The groups are obedience-based, not knowledge-focused. Follow Jesus by learning and obeying the Bible through the guidance of the Holy Spirit. Make practical and specific commitments each meeting and review them the next time you meet. Become "fishers of people" by training others how to learn and obey as well. This creates an environment in which loving Jesus means obeying Jesus.

Discuss and Discover
Focus on the Bible. Trust the Holy Spirit to help each person discover the meaning of Scripture. Lead through asking questions rather than preaching.

Appendix C: Core Practices Mentor Guide

Leader/Mentor Phase What the mentor does	Model Mentor gives direction and information	Assist Mentor gives direction and support	Watch Mentor gives support and encouragement	Leave Mentor stays connected and receives updates
Discipleship Phase What the disciple under-stands and does	D1 I don't understand it or do it	D2 I understand and do it, but need help	D3 I understand and do it, but I may have questions	D4 I fully understand and regularly practice it; no help needed
The Core Practices				
Love God Hear God, grow your faith and respond in obedience				
Self-feed:	—	—	—	—
Read Scripture daily				
Pray (talk/listen)				
Resist the enemy, prepare for persecution				
Be accountable with one-to-two others				

Leader/Mentor Phase What the mentor does	Model Mentor gives direction and information	Assist Mentor gives direction and support	Watch Mentor gives support and encourgement	Leave Mentor stays connected and receives updates
Discipleship Phase What the disciple understands and does	D1	D2	D3	D4
	I don't understand it or do it	I understand and do it, but need help	I understand and do it, but I may have questions	I fully understand and regularly practice it; no help needed
The Core Practices				
Love People				
Stay connected with your discipler (duckling)				
Be a simple church:	—	—	—	—
Fellowship				
Practice the "one-anothers" (body life)				
Read and know the Bible (obey and train)				
Celebrate Communion				
Give (time and money)				

Leader/Mentor Phase	Model	Assist	Watch	Leave
What the mentor does	Mentor gives direction and information	Mentor gives direction and support	Mentor gives support and encouragement	Mentor stays connected and receives updates
Discipleship Phase	D1	D2	D3	D4
What the disciple understands and does	I don't understand it or do it	I understand and do it, but need help	I understand and do it, but I may have questions	I fully understand and regularly practice it; no help needed
The Core Practices	—	—	—	—
Make Disciples				
Look for where the Kingdom isn't				
Prayer-walk, look for persons of peace				
Tell your story, tell God's story				
Steward relationships (list of twenty or one hundred)				
Baptize new believers				
Lead 3/3 groups (obey, train, share)				
Be a part of two churches				
MAWL with your disciple(s)				

Endnotes

Introduction and Definitions

1. Bart Ehrman, *The Triumph of Christianity: How a Forbidden Religion Swept the World*, (New York: Simon & Schuster, 2019), p. 4.
2. See Acts 9:2.
3. *Strong's Greek: 5083. Τηρέω (Téreó) -- to watch over, to guard*, https://biblehub.com/greek/5083.htm.

Chapter 1 — It's Not Working

1. See David Olson, *The American Church in Crisis: Groundbreaking Research Based on a National Database of Over 200,000 Churches* (Grand Rapids; Zondervan, 2008), especially chapter 3.
2. David Olson, *The American Church in Crisis*, loc. 1581.
3. David Olson, *The American Church in Crisis*, loc. 1780. This figure is for the period 1999–2005. A 2017 study by researcher Thom Rainer indicated that 35 percent of churches are growing: *Dispelling the 80 Percent Myth of Declining Churches* (see https://thomrainer.com/2017/06/dispelling-80-percent-myth-declining-churches).
4. See George Barna, *Is Evangelism Going Out of Style?*, 2013 (https://www.barna.com/research/is-evangelism-going-out-of-style). This is despite the fact that 73 percent of born again Christians (and 100 percent of evangelicals) stated a personal responsibility to share their faith with others.
5. See Joe Carter, *Study: Most Churchgoers Never Share the Gospel*, 2012 (https://www.thegospelcoalition.org/article/study-most-churchgoers-never-share-the-gospel). This study reflects American adults who attend a Protestant church once a month or more.
6. See Ed Stetzer, "The Epidemic of Bible Illiteracy in Our Churches," *Christianity Today*, July 2015 (https://www.christianitytoday.com/edstetzer/2015/july/epidemic-of-bible-illiteracy-in-our-churches.html).
7. See Barna Group, *Most American Christians Do Not Believe that Satan or the Holy Spirit Exist*, 2009 (https://www.barna.com/research/most-american-christians-do-not-believe-that-satan-or-the-holy-spirit-exist).
8. See David Kinnaman, *Christians: More Like Jesus or Pharisees?*, https://www.barna.com/research/christians-more-like-jesus-or-pharisees).

9. See David Kinnaman, *unChristian: What a New Generation Really Thinks about Christianity...and Why It Matters* (Ada, MI: Baker Books, 2012), p. 26–27.

10. See Matt. 28:19–21.

11. See Matt. 7:21–27, Luke 6:46, John 14:15, 14:21, Heb. 4:1–2, 1 John 2:3–6, among many others.

12. Rhodes, Ron. *The Complete Guide to Christian Denominations.* Harvest House Publishers, Eugene, OR: 2015, p. 12.

13. See John 17:20–21.

14. See Acts 15:36–41.

Chapter 2 — Paradigms and Perceptions

1. Stephen Covey, *The 7 Habits of Highly Effective People: Powerful Lessons in Personal Change* (New York, NY: Fireside, 1990), pp. 23–29.

2. See Nicholls, M.E.R., Churches, O. & Loetscher, T. Perception of an ambiguous figure is affected by own-age social biases. *Sci Rep* 8, 12661 (2018). https://doi.org/10.1038/s41598-018-31129-7, and Shakhnaz-arova, N. (2018, September 21). Whether you see a young or old woman in this classic optical illusion may depend on your age, researchers say. Retrieved August 05, 2020, from https://www.thesun.co.uk/news/7307450/optical-illusion-young-or-old-woman-depends-on-age.

3. Covey, pp. 28–29.

4. See Acts 1:15.

Chapter 3 — How We Got Here

1. Philip Schaff, *History of the Christian Church*, 8 vols. (Peabody: Hendrickson, 2006), loc. 14770.

2. Schaff, *History of the Christian Church*, loc. 12711.

3. Schaff, *History of the Christian Church*, loc. 12395.

4. Everett Ferguson, *Church History Vol. One: From Christ to the Pre-Reformation* (Grand Rapids: Zondervan), p. 172. See also James Robertson, *Sketches of Church History From A.D 33 to the Reformation* (New York, The Tract Commit-tee, 1887), loc. 24. See also William Frend, *St. Cyprian: Christian Theologian and Bishop*, Encyclopædia Britannica, https://www.britannica.com/biography/Saint-Cyprian-Christian-bishop.

5. Schaff, *History of the Christian Church*, loc. 12380.

6. Turtullian, Apologeticus, Chapter 50.

7. Schaff, *History of the Christian Church*, loc. 13900.

8. Ferguson, *Church History*, p. 212.
9. Schaff, *History of the Christian Church*, loc. 27151. Note: Ferguson, *Church History*, p. 212, lists Caesarea instead of Constantinople.
10. Schaff, *History of the Christian Church*, loc. 24844.
11. Schaff, *History of the Christian Church*, loc. 25064.
12. Ferguson, *Church History*, p. 234ff.
13. Schaff, *History of the Christian Church*, loc. 25271.
14. Schaff, *History of the Christian Church*, loc. 24884.
15. Schaff, *History of the Christian Church*, loc. 24844.
16. Schaff, *History of the Christian Church*, loc. 23892.
17. Schaff, *History of the Christian Church*, loc. 26694.
18. Schaff, *History of the Christian Church*, loc. 26712.
19. Schaff, *History of the Christian Church*, loc. 403.
20. Ferguson, *Church History*, p. 322–323.
21. Schaff, *History of the Christian Church*, loc. 36852.
22. Ferguson, *Church History*, p. 227.
23. Schaff, *History of the Christian Church*, loc. 23781.
24. Schaff, *History of the Christian Church*, loc. 25954.
25. Ferguson, *Church History*, p. 426.
26. Ferguson, *Church History*, p. 334.
27. Ferguson, *Church History*, p. 335.
28. Ferguson, *Church History*, p. 368–369.
29. Ferguson, *Church History*, p. 418.
30. Schaff, *History of the Christian Church*, loc. 39743.
31. Ferguson, *Church History*, p. 401.
32. Schaff, *History of the Christian Church*, loc. 421.
33. Ferguson, *Church History*, p. 426.
34. Schaff, *History of the Christian Church*, loc. 55250.
35. Ferguson, *Church History*, p. 430, 485. See also Schaff, *History of the Christian Church*, loc. 53901.
36. Ferguson, *Church History*, p. 521.
37. Gianozzo Manetti, *On the Dignity and Excellence of Man*, cited in Clare, J., *Italian Renaissance*. See "Renaissance." Wikipedia, Wikimedia Foundation, 28 Dec. 2019, https://en.wikipedia.org/wiki/Renaissance#cite_note-50.
38. Schaff, *History of the Christian Church*, loc. 66663.
39. See Schaff, *History of the Christian Church*, loc. 58501.
40. Schaff, *History of the Christian Church*, loc. 66913, 69730, 69751.

41. Schaff, *History of the Christian Church*, loc. 66931, 66411.

42. Schaff, *History of the Christian Church*, loc. 69973.

43. Schaff, *History of the Christian Church*, loc. 66449.

44. Schaff, *History of the Christian Church*, loc. 75814, 76046.

45. Schaff, *History of the Christian Church*, loc. 70138, 70159, 76125, 70391, 70430, 76146, 76478.

46. Jason Daley, *Researchers Catalogue the Grisly Deaths of Soldiers in the Thirty Years' War*, Smithsonian. See also Schaff, *History of the Christian Church*, loc. 307.

47. Schaff, *History of the Christian Church*, loc. 70200.

48. Schaff, *History of the Christian Church*, loc. 70221.

49. Mark Noll, *The Rise of Evangelicalism: The Age of Edwards, Whitefield and the Wesleys* (Downers Grove: IVP Academic, 2018), p. 33–37.

50. For example, see Beeke, Joel. "Prayer Meetings and Revival in the Church": The Grand Awakening, http://www.grandawakening.org/great-article-on-prayer-and-revival.html.

51. Augustus Cerillo, *The Beginnings of American Pentecostalism: A Historiographical Overview* (1999), cited in Blumhofer, Edith Waldvogel., et al. *Pentecostal Currents in American Protestantism*. University of Illinois Press, 2004, pp. 229–260.

52. McLouglin, William Gerald. *Revivals, Awakenings, and Reform: An Essay on Religion and Social Change in America*, 1607–1977. The Univ. of Chicago Press, 1989.

Chapter 4 — Multiplication: What and Why

1. "List of Megachurches in the United States." Wikipedia, Wikimedia Foundation, 22 Dec. 2019, https://en.wikipedia.org/wiki/List_of_megachurches_in_the_United_States. Note: As of this publication this article has been tagged as requiring updated information. However, for the purposes of use in this illustration the data is relevant.

2. "U.S. and World Population Clock." Population Clock, U.S. Census Bureau, https://www.census.gov/popclock. Retrieved Dec. 27, 2019.

3. "Nevada and Idaho Are the Nation's Fastest-Growing States." The United States Census Bureau, U.S. Census Bureau, 20 Dec. 2018, https://www.census.gov/newsroom/press-releases/2018/estimates-national-state.html.

4. Outreach Magazine. "7 Startling Facts: An Up Close Look at Church Attendance in America." ChurchLeaders, *Outreach Magazine*, 10 Apr. 2018, https://

churchleaders.com/pastors/pastor-articles/139575-7-startling-facts-an-up-close-look-at-church-attendance-in-america.html/4.

5. Outreach Magazine. "7 Startling Facts: An Up Close Look at Church Attendance in America." ChurchLeaders, *Outreach Magazine*, 10 Apr. 2018, https://churchleaders.com/pastors/pastor-articles/139575-7-startling-facts-an-up-close-look-at-church-attendance-in-america.html/2.

6. Rainer, Thom. "Major New Research on Declining, Plateaued, and Growing Churches from Exponential and LifeWay Research." ThomRainer.com, 16 Dec. 2019, https://thomrainer.com/2019/03/major-new-research-on-declining-plateaued-and-growing-churches-from-exponential-and-lifeway-research.

7. "Small, Struggling Congregations Fill U.S. Church Landscape." LifeWay Research, 6 Mar. 2019, https://lifewayresearch.com/2019/03/06/small-struggling-congregations-fill-u-s-church-landscape/.
See also Rainer, Thom. "Major New Research on Declining, Plateaued and Growing Churches." ChurchLeaders, 7 June 2019, https://churchleaders.com/pastors/pastor-articles/346486-major-new-research-on-declining-plateaued-and-growing-churches.html.

8. "America's Changing Religious Landscape." Pew Research Center's Religion & Public Life Project, 12 May 2015, https://www.pewforum.org/2015/05/12/americas-changing-religious-landscape/.

9. "The Art of Spiritual Conversation in a Changing Culture." Barna Group, 17 June 2013, https://www.barna.com/research/the-art-of-spiritual-conversation-in-a-changing-culture.

10. "America's Changing Religious Landscape." Pew Research Center's Religion & Public Life Project, 12 May 2015, https://www.pewforum.org/2015/05/12/americas-changing-religious-landscape/.

11. See "Almost Half of Practicing Christian Millennials Say Evangelism Is Wrong." Barna Group, 5 Feb. 2019, https://www.barna.com/research/millennials-oppose-evangelism.

12. *24:14 Movement Data Dashboard*, May 2019.

Chapter 5 — What the Church Is

1. As a point of reference, my theological background is dispensational in focus; my primary church experience was a non-denominational Bible church.

2. See Paul and Barnabas in Acts 15.

3. For more insight and examples on this topic, see *Creativity, Inc.: Overcoming the Unseen Forces That Stand in the Way of True Inspiration*. Random House,

Inc., 2014. Also see McChrystal, Stanley A., et al. *Team of Teams: New Rules of Engagement For a Complex World*. Portfolio/Penguin, 2015.

4. Brafman, Ori, and Rod A. Beckstrom. *The Starfish and the Spider: The Unstoppable Power of Leaderless Organizations*. Penguin Putnam Inc, 2008.

5. For more discussion on this from the perspective of servant leadership see *Contrast #12 – Leadership: Professional Clergy vs. Bivocational Leader* [page 128].

Chapter 6 — What the Church Does

1. See chapter 3 and the impact of the Enlightenment on the form and function of the church in Western Europe.

2. For a helpful description of both "lag" and "lead" metrics and the role they play in accomplishing organizational objectives, see McChesney, Chris, et al. *The 4 Disciplines of Execution: Achieving Your Wildly Important Goals*. Free Press, 2012.

3. See the Core Practices Mentor Guide in Appendix C.

4. Groups transition to home churches when the following elements are in place: identified leader(s), the reading and study of the Bible, worship, baptism, prayer, fellowship, sharing of resources and serving each other, commemorating the Lord's Supper in communion and telling others about Jesus. For more explanation see *Contrast #11 – Primary Meeting Structure: Congregation vs. Small Group* [page 123].

Chapter 7 — How the Church is Led and Developed

1. See Brown, Colin. *The New International Dictionary of New Testament Theology*, Volume 1. Regency Reference Library, 1986, pp. 190–192.

2. Strong's Greek: 4291. Προΐστημι (*Proistemi*) -- I Rule, https://biblehub.com/greek/4291.htm.

3. See Brown, *The New International Dictionary of New Testament Theology*, Volume 1, pp. 164–169.

4. See Jas. 2:14–19.

5. For further context, *ginosko* was the word used in such passages as John 17:3 ("Now this is eternal life: that they know you, the only true God, and Jesus Christ, whom you have sent."), Ephesians 3:19 ("...to know this love that surpasses knowledge—that you may be filled to the measure of all the fullness of God."), Philippians 3:10 ("I want to know Christ—yes, to know the power of his resurrection and participation in his sufferings..."), 1 John 2:13 ("I am writing to you, fathers, because you know him who is from the beginning.").

Other Greek words translated as "know" in the New Testament usually carry different emphases, such as *eidó* (be aware, behold, consider, perceive), *oida* (to have seen or perceived), *epistemai* (to understand, being acquainted with, know about), and *suneidon* (to see together, to comprehend).

6. Some have argued that the gift of apostleship was limited to Jesus' original disciples and thus no longer valid for the church past the apostolic age. This view does not take into account the broader use of the term "apostle" (lit. "one sent on a mission," "messenger," or "delegate"). Others in the New Testament were called "apostles" and functioned as such (see Acts 14:4, 14; Rom. 16:7; 1 Cor. 9:6, 15:7; Gal. 1:19; cf. 1 Cor. 4:6, 9; 1 Thess. 1:1; 2:7). The word *apostolos* also describes any servant who is sent by his master on any mission (John 13:16).

7. For further discussion on the APEST gifts (and particularly the role of the apostolic gift), see Hirsch, Alan. *Forgotten Ways: Reactivating Apostolic Movements.* Ada, MI. Baker Publishing Group, 2016.

Chapter 8 — How the Church Engages With People

1. Pink, Daniel H. *Drive: The Surprising Truth About What Motivates Us.* New York, NY. Riverhead Books, 2011.

Chapter 9 — How People Engage with the Church

1. See John 8:55.

Chapter 11 — Strategies & Implications

1. See http://wigtakedmm.com/bless.
2. See http://wigtakedmm.com/release.
3. Galanos, Chris. *From Megachurch to Multiplication: A Church's Journey Toward Movement.* Experience Life, 2018.
4. Garrison, V. David. *Church Planting Movements: How God Is Redeeming a Lost World.* WIGTake Resources, 2004.
5. Moran, Roy. *Spent Matches: Igniting the Signal Fire for the Spiritually Dissatisfied.* Thomas Nelson, 2015.
6. Moran, Roy. *Spent Matches*, p. 141.

Chapter 12 — Changing the Church

1. Kotter, John P. *Leading Change.* Harvard Business Review Press, 2012.

2. Smith, Steve. *The Spirit Walk: The Extraordinary Power of Acts for Ordinary People*. 2414 Ventures, 2018.

3. Sergeant, Curtis. *The Only One: Living Fully In, By, and for God.* Pasadena, CA. William Carey Library Publishing, 2018.

4. Sputo, Dominic. *Heirloom Love: Authentic Christianity for This Age of Persecution*. Lakeland, FL. LumenLife, 2018.

5. Sputo, Dominic, and Smith, Brian. *Heirloom Love (Small Group Study)*. Lakeland, FL. LumenLife, 2018.

About the Author

Damian Gerke is called to help individuals and churches experience genuine transformation into the identity of Jesus through following him in faith and living out his teachings. He is part of the leadership team of 1Body Church, a network of disciple-making simple churches based in Tampa, Florida.

He is also a learning and performance practitioner, a leadership coach, and author. He has worked as a pastor, in the marketplace, and as a professional coach, helping countless people in a variety of roles understand and apply the principles of effective leadership in practical, actionable ways.

He is a Certified Professional in Learning and Performance (CPLP) through the Association for Talent Development, as well as a credentialed member (ACC) of the International Coaching Federation.

Damian is the author of *Taking the Lead: What Riding a Bike Can Teach You About Leadership*. He blogs regularly about leadership and life issues at DamianGerke.com, as well as faith and church leadership issues at 1body.church.

Made in the USA
Las Vegas, NV
19 February 2021